Phenomenology and the Metaphysics of Presence

PHAENOMENOLOGICA

COLLECTION FONDÉE PAR H. L. VAN BREDA ET PUBLIÉE SOUS LE
PATRONAGE DES CENTRES D'ARCHIVES-HUSSERL

69

WOLFGANG WALTER FUCHS

Phenomenology and the Metaphysics of Presence

WOLFGANG WALTER FUCHS

Phenomenology and the Metaphysics of Presence

AN ESSAY IN THE PHILOSOPHY OF EDMUND HUSSERL

MARTINUS NIJHOFF / THE HAGUE / 1976

I wish to acknowledge the support I received from the
Faculty Research Committee of Towson State College for the
preparation of the manuscript.

ISBN 90 247 1822 8

PRINTED IN THE NETHERLANDS

TABLE OF CONTENTS

CHAPTER I

INTRODUCTION: PHENOMENOLOGY AND THE BEGINNING

Phenomenology begins in the work of Edmund Husserl; the first of his phenomenological publications was the *Logische Untersuchungen* of 1901. It is rare that the beginning point of a philosophical movement can be identified with such precision. We must take advantage of this fortunate circumstance in order to better understand the phenomenological movement, for the notions of "origin" and "beginning" themselves play a key part in the development of the phenomenological teaching.

Being able to pinpoint the beginning of phenomenology is not to deny that Husserl had philosophical predecessors or that he had been influenced by other thinkers. To the contrary, Husserl acknowledges his debt to people like Franz Brentano and Paul Natrop. Also, from the perspective of history he sees what he calls the incipient phenomenology of Descartes, Hume, Kant, and others, who *do* phenomenology to some extent without realizing the consequences, thereby losing the thread and falling away from their "phenomenology."

To read the history of philosophy and be able to recognize similarity in the direction of certain philosophical thinking is not, however, the same thing as tracing back to the origins of one's own thought; Husserl begins phenomenology in its self-consciousness, and phenomenology depends upon this abrupt or radical sort of beginning. According to Husserl the idea of a radical beginning is necessarily tied to the philosophical enterprise:

Must not the demand for a philosophy aiming at the ultimate conceivable freedom from prejudice, shaping itself with actual autonomy according to ultimate evidences it has itself produced, and therefore absolutely self-responsible – must not this demand, instead of being excessive, be part of the fundamental sense of genuine philosophy?[1]

Phenomenology then depends upon the return to the beginning in the sense that philosophers must rid themselves of their prejudices and must overthrow the dependence on previous philosophies as sources of knowledge. But there is also another sense in which phenomenology is associated in a special way with the notion of beginning. Every systematically developed complex of thought or knowledge moves through mediation from its foundations to greater and more intricate levels of knowledge. It is important therefore that the foundation of the system of knowledge be secured and be understood, since the entire edifice is threatened if the foundation is weak or unintelligible. Much of the work of Husserl is the effort at the grounding of the sciences and of knowledge in general, in order that the systematic development of *Wissenschaft* be on firm foundations, foundations which have themselves been examined and comprehended. In this way too phenomenology is concerned with the notion of origin.

Finally, there is yet another way in which the return to beginnings plays a role in phenomenology. Husserl himself consistently returned to the beginning moments of his own philosophic work, constantly reexamining *his* beginnings. What is perhaps most admirable about Husserl as a philosopher is that he is perpetually the "beginning philosopher." In his own intellectual work Husserl follows many times the suggestion he makes to philosophers in the *Cartesian Meditations*:

First, anyone who seriously intends to become a philosopher must "once in his life" withdraw into himself and attempt, within himself, to overthrow and build anew all the sciences that, up to then, he has been accepting. Philosophy – wisdom – is the philosophizer's quite personal affair.[2]

In spite of all this scrutiny however we find in our return to the beginning of phenomenology that there was not achieved the radical break with the history of philosophy that Husserl thought he had accomplished. In fact, we find that the "beginning" made by Husserl is very much in keeping with what might be the oldest and most dominant trend in the history of western philosophical

[1] Edmund Husserl, *Cartesian Meditations*, trans. D. Cairns (The Hague: Martinus Nijhoff, 1960), p. 6.
[2] *Ibid.*, p. 2.

thinking, a trend which we elaborate as the "metaphysics of presence."

It is always possible in retrospect to see prejudices that could not have been seen at the initiation of a "new" beginning of philosophy. Perhaps this indicates that the notions of "origin" and "beginning" themselves must be subject to criticism. From the perspective of history Husserl found it possible to reflect on the meaning of Descartes' attempt at a radical beginning, and found unstated presuppositions that needed to be unearthed. Of course we too speak from the perspective of history, and in part our effort too is that of attempting to reclaim the beginning of phenomenology in order to rid it of *its* inarticulated and thoroughly diffused presuppositions. And we shall do so by returning to the origin of phenomenology, the work of Edmund Husserl.

Taking *Ideas* as the central (but not definitive) work in the Husserlean development of phenomenology we find that Husserl elaborates an epistemology that incorporates that traditional orientation of western philosophy which we call the metaphysics of presence.

This is a problematic already located and identified by Jacques Derrida in his interesting and important work *Speech and Phenomena*, where he discovers this orientation at work within Husserl's theory of signs:

> The historic destiny of phenomenology seems in any case to be contained in these two motifs: on the one hand, phenomenology is the reduction of naive ontology, the return to an active constitution of sense and value, to the activity of a *life* which produces truth and value in general through its signs. But at the same time, without being simply juxtaposed to this move, another factor will necessarily confirm the classical metaphysics of presence and indicate the adherence of phenomenology to classical ontology. It is with this adherence that we have chosen to interest ourselves.[3]

Husserl does not anywhere justify this orientation; it just never occurs to him to question it. Throughout his teaching in *Ideas* we see that being in the mode of presence is given a privileged place; it constitutes the epistemological and metaphysical moment, the high-point of philosophical activity. It is in terms of this that the radical intuitionist thesis of Husserl must be understood in order

[3] Jacques Derrida, *Speech and Phenomena* and Other Essays on Husserl's Theory of Signs, trans. D. Allison (Evanston: Northwestern University Press, 1973), pp. 25–6.

to be appreciated in its fullest sense. Furthermore, all of the major themes of Husserl's thinking: the *Wesesschau*, the phenomenological epoché, *Sinngebung*, evidence, all function within this classical notion, the metaphysical and epistemological priority of presence. In the second chapter we show how this concept is operative in *Ideas* by giving an interpretation in terms of it, thereby articulating the most fundamental epistemological teachings of Husserl in that work.

This notion of the metaphysical priority of presence, however, comes into conflict with some of the most famous phenomenological descriptions and analyses worked out by Husserl himself. We shall examine three of these descriptions that are at the very heart of Husserl's phenomenological teaching: language, time, and intersubjectivity. And we find that in all of these cases, the work of Husserl himself shows the illegitimacy of the doctrine that contends the primacy of presence.

We examine the doctrine of language as presented in the *Logische Untersuchungen* and we see that nowhere does Husserl acknowledge the *density* of language, that aspect of the being of language whereby concepts and words operate in terms of each other, and not simply independently or clearly. For Husserl, however, consciousness becomes aware of self-constituted meanings. But to maintain this is to neglect the reality of language as a system which resists being reduced to a series of meanings constituted by consciousness.

Husserl's desire is to understand language within the realm of the metaphysics of presence, and it is this desire that makes him overlook the complexity of the phenomenon of language. In the end, it is Husserl himself who reveals this to us when we see how language is tied up with the phenomenological concept of evidence. It is here that Husserl shows that his concept of language is inadequate since in order to account for the relation of language and evidence Husserl has to lapse into ambiguity concerning the nature of language. That ambiguity revolves around the relationship of the presence of meaning as dependent upon the absent system of meanings and words.

Of all of the specific doctrines of Husserl the teaching on time is probably the most influential. Husserl has an explication of time that is unique in the history of philosophy, and this is taken up and "exploded" by the existentialists who come after him. But what is seized upon by those who followed him is not exactly what Husserl intended. Contrary to his own desires, Husserl shows that in originary temporality *de*-presentation is as original as presentation. The past and the future are not present, and yet they, no less than the present itself, function originarily in the constitution of time. That means that absence is co-primordial with presence, a thesis that is in direct contradiction to the teaching of the primacy of being in the mode of presence.

This same theme is followed out in our examination of Husserl's doctrine of intersubjectivity. There have been may critics who have claimed that Husserl fails to resolve the problematic of the meaning of the existence of the Other, and we are in agreement with those critics. What is of interest, however, is to think through the source of that failure and to find that it centers around the attempt to reduce the alien to presence. Husserl finds himself in the dilemma that he must either abandon his transcendental idealism (which we see as a manifestation of the metaphysics of presence) or he is condemned to a type of solipsism, a position which he himself declared to be absurd. We find that either there must be granted the co-primordiality of absence and presence, or there is lost the otherness of the Other. And this, the otherness of the Other, is precisely the phenomenon we are trying to explicate. In the teaching of Husserl this remains unresolved in the end since he does not abandon the metaphysics of presence.

In retrospect we see that Husserl has not been freed of all presuppositions and prejudices. To the contrary, it is to one of the very oldest that he is subject, the metaphysics of presence; the teaching that the presence to being *is* the metaphysical moment. But we realize this inarticulated dependency because in his descriptions of the phenomena of time, language, and the Other, Husserl himself reveals the necessity of understanding presence and absence as co-primordial if an account is to be given of the "things themselves." Ultimately therefore it is in the work of Husserl himself that we ground our phenomenological research.

CHAPTER II

EPISTEMOLOGY AND THE METAPHYSICS
OF PRESENCE

A. THE METAPHYSICS OF PRESENCE

Western philosophy follows out a line of what Jacques Derrida has named the metaphysics of presence. The movement of that great thought which began with the Greeks and culminated in Hegel was the idea of metaphysics, the science of Being *qua* Being. What is of interest here is that this great thought moved in a certain direction, along a certain theme – that the metaphysical moment is the moment of presence; that the metaphysical notion of Being as it is in itself is the notion of absolute presence. The general doctrine of the metaphysics of presence can be summed up in the following way:

1. Being, as the most universal concept, defies definition in terms of lower concepts. But this is also true of the concept of presence. The metaphysics of presence maintains that entities participate in Being, that they do not exhaust Being and that they do not delimit Being. Exactly the same thought is carried through about presence in regard to entities. Entities are present in Being, their presence is the manifestation of Being, but their absence is not a delimitation of Being, since there is always the presence of other entities to manifest Being, to bring Being to presence. This means that Being is absolute; it is not relative to entities or to conceptual determinations. Precisely here we can see that presence is a mode of Being, and in the metaphysics of presence, the supreme metaphysical moment is when Being reveals itself, presents itself as Being-in-the-mode-of-presence.

2. The real nexus of the concepts of Being and presence is to be found in temporality in the concept of "the present." Being is given in the absolute present moment because Being is eternal,

trans-temporal, and therefore primarily present. That which is not in the present is not given as being in a primary mode of Being. That which was, for example, is given in the mode of having-been. That which is in the present is what is, that is, manifests Being through its presence in the present.

3. Being is absolute. Being is that other than which nothing is. The limit of Being is nonbeing; it is the ground of all mediation. Nonbeing and absence are derivative, mediated categories. Being-in-the-mode-of-presence is absolute presence.

4. The notion of Being as absolute presence means that Being in itself, the eternal, immutable idea of Being, is the notion of absolute presence, and therefore the exclusion of the notions of the temporal, the incomplete, and the negative. The notion of Being, in its primordial manifestation is the exclusion of absence. These are the thoughts that are at the heart of that line of thinking in Western philosophy which is the metaphysics of presence.

Already in Plato's analogy of the cave this metaphysical notion of Being is delimited and defined by contrast with the notion of absence. All persons, save only the philosopher, are doomed to be dealing only with shadows, the phantom, and to think that it is the real. But even those who see outside of the cave, through the exercise of reason, see only shadows at first. Of course they are the shadows of the real world, not of the cave, but they are shadows nonetheless. They are mere profiles; they have no depth, no substantial being.

After some time, Plato tells us, it would be possible to look directly at the things of the world themselves, no longer being restricted to mere reflections. But even to see these beings as they are is not yet the exercise of the philosophical act, not yet the metaphysical moment. For what is not given in the vision of these things of the world is their source, the ground of their being. That is to say, Being *qua* Being has not yet been given – Being in the mode of absolute presence. The entities of the world are temporal, unstable, constantly changing, that is, not in absolute presence. The last thing to be perceived is the good itself, in the analogy of the cave, the sun. And this vision is given all at once; it is unchanging, unadumbrated, the eternal source and ground of all being and all change. For it to be grasped all at once, to be grasped in a single vision means that it is given as *presence*, absolute, total, and complete. It is this moment of presence which is for Plato the metaphysical moment. Plato tells us that it is only after having this vision that one has become a philosopher, has comprehended Being *qua* Being.

We see also in Hegel this theme of the metaphysics of presence. The moment of Being *qua* Being is the presence of Spirit to itself, all at once, no longer history, no longer becoming, no longer mediated. As in the thought of Plato, so too in the thought of Hegel, Being is presence, and the metaphysical moment that creates philosophy is the direct presence of Being, enduring, timeless, and absolute.

As a final example of a philosophy which is grounded in the metaphysics of presence let us consider the aim of the work of Kant – the destruction of metaphysics. How is it possible to consider him within this tradition? Paradoxically, it is perhaps most clear with Kant, who limits reason and declares classical metaphysics to be impossible, just what is at the heart of this type of thought which we call the metaphysics of presence. The most fundamental epistemological and metaphysical reason why metaphysics is impossible, says Kant, is because there is no way to know the things-in-themselves; there is no way that the human reason can come into the presence of the things themselves. Metaphysics is impossible *because* Being cannot come into presence; all that is possible is Appearance, which is precisely *other than* the presence of Being itself.

It is only on the ground of this understanding of metaphysics that it makes sense for Kant to claim that metaphysics is indeed impossible, that it goes beyond the limit of human knowledge in its claims. But this means that Kant has exactly the same notion of the metaphysical moment as do Plato and Hegel – that Being is presence. Kant, in denying metaphysics, affirms completely the highest aspirations of metaphysics.

Following Kant, Husserl too aimed at a philosophy free of presuppositions by means of pursuing a radical positivism in an epistemological investigation. But, in fact, his radical positivism presupposes a certain metaphysics – precisely that classical one which we have called the metaphysics of presence. With this conclusion as the guiding thought we shall give an interpretation of Husserl's central work, *Ideen I*, showing how this metaphysical notion reveals itself through three major themes in Husserl's work.

1. That intuition is the epistemological foundation of true positivism.

2. That the transcendental sphere is the sphere of Being.

3. That Being giving itself in intuition is the epistemological moment for Husserl. This means Being is absolute presence – that is, the metaphysical moment.

In this way we shall see that Husserl does indeed have a presupposition, the metaphysics of presence.

B. POSITIVISM

Paul Ricoeur has called Kant our "oldest contemporary." The resolute intention to avoid "mere metaphysical speculation," in favor of a type of positivism, contemporary philosophy owes to Kant. Taking the research and principles of British Empiricism seriously, Kant is determined to elaborate an epistemology which grounds itself in the principle that all knowledge begins in experience. Kantian empiricism maintains that the source of all possible experience lies in sensible intuition.

> Objects are *given* to us by means of sensibility, and it alone yields us intuitions; they are thought through the understanding, and from the understanding arises concepts.[1]

This passage expresses the very foundation of Kant's epistemology, since it is here that he acknowledges that objects are given to intuition. But we can also see here an ontological corollary. The sensibility, through which we are part of Nature for Kant, is the ontological ground of the epistemological operations because it is the locus of the givenness of being. Epistemologically and ontologically, the presence of being is accomplished through the sensibility. It is on this foundation, however, that for Kant the metaphysical moment is impossible, as we have noted above.

Husserl has taken up the spirit of the epistemological teaching of Kant and the ontological doctrine which is its necessary correlate. But in taking up this spirit, Husserl has, as we shall see,

---

[1] Immanuel Kant, *Critique of Pure Reason*, trans. N.K. Smith (New York: St. Martins, 1965), p. 33.

radicalized this teaching to bring about a new epistemological and ontological understanding of intuition, And in this radicalization Husserl in fact moves to rejoin the dominating thrust of Western metaphysics: the metaphysics of presence. The major preoccupation of Husserl, and the result of his work, is the development of an epistemology which reveals that cognition is cognition of Being in the mode of presence. In Husserl, the end result of his radical epistemology is nothing less than a rejuvenation of the Western philosophical tradition which teaches that Being, in its most fundamental mode, is Presence.

In seeking a truly positivist epistemology Husserl establishes a rigorous criterion of knowledge; we shall see that for him the *only* ultimately validating criterion of knowledge is that evidence which is self-evidence, that which is obtained through direct intuition, that is, an intuition of the object in its "bodily presence." This notion of self-evidence is one which Husserl worked on very diligently and which we shall discuss further in the chapter on language. What is important here is the realization that Husserl carries through this notion of self-evidence as *the* criterion which validates knowledge. Of course not all cognition is immediately given in this way, nor even immediately evidenced as such; there is also "founded knowledge," knowledge that is not achieved by a direct intuition and even that which is not intuitive at all. But, it is the task of what Husserl calls intentional analysis to trace the founded back to the original founding intuition, since all knowledge is ultimately derived from, and is of, objects given through intuition. This means that in principle such analysis must always be possible, and that "returning" to such intuition provides immediate evidence for knowledge. It is nothing less radical than this that he means when he says in *The Idea of Phenomenology:*

> It will not do to draw conclusions from existences of which one knows but which one cannot "see." "Seeing" does not lend itself to demonstration or deduction. It is patently absurd to try to explain possibilities (and unmediated possibilities at that) by drawing logical conclusions from non-intuitive knowledge.[2]

In carrying through the positivist standpoint Husserl demands that knowledge on all levels be grounded in epistemological pre-

[2] Edmund Husserl, *The Idea of Phenonemology*, trans. Alston and Nakhnikian (The Hague: Martinus Nijhoff, 1964), p. 2.

sence. It is through intentional analysis that Husserl shows how *all* knowledge is founded on direct intuition. It is the aim of this chapter to give an expository account of the direction of Husserl's thought as it moves within this guiding principle, and to show that he has a teaching in which all phenomena of this type are brought to epistemological presence, as well as the corollary onto-logical doctrine that what is given in intuition is true Being. That is, what is brought into epistemological presence is onto-logically fundamental.

That the founding intuitions are the absolute criteria for the knowledge of what is, is what lies at the heart of what Husserl calls (and uses as) the principle of all principles:

> No theory we can conceive can mislead us in regard to the principle of all principles: that every primordial dator intuition is a source of authority for knowledge, that whatever presents itself in "intuition" in primordial form (as it were in its bodily reality), is simply to be accepted as it gives itself out to be, though only within the limits in which it then presents itself.[3]

Already implied here are two ways in which Husserl carries through a more radical positivism than Kant. (1) It is true that Kant maintains that all knowledge begins with experience, but he also maintains that it does not follow that it all arises out of experience, and therefore certainly not out of intuition. Husserl, however, maintains that all knowledge does in fact arise out of intuition, that intuition *is* the source of all knowledge. (2) For Kant, all intuitions are sensible intuitions. They are the intuitions of the faculty of the sensibility which have as their objects sensible data. This is for Kant the only type of intuition possible. Husserl claims not only sensible intuitions which have as their ob-jects sensible data, but also eidetic intuitions, intuitions of es-sences. This is the famous *"Wesensschau."* Let us take up first the possible types of intuitions and their possible objects.

C. INTUITION

It is a fundamental axiom of phenomenology that every act of consciousness is an intentional act; that all consciousness is con-

---

[3] Edmund Husserl, *Ideas: General Introduction to Pure Phenomenology*, trans. Gibson (London: George Allen and Unwin, 1933), p. 32.

sciousness of ... This means that every act of consciousness has an *object*. An object need not be a spatio-temporal thing since Husserl explicitly uses the term in the sense of formal logic where an object is "every subject of possibly true predications."[4] There are, says Husserl, different types of objects just as there are different types of acts of consciousness. Imagining has as its object the imagined object, remembering the object remembered, wishing the object wished, etc.

One of the acts of consciousness is intuition. As we have already seen, it is the teaching of Kant, in keeping with the spirit of positivism, that knowledge is obtained first of all by means of sensible intuitions. For Husserl too the fact of sensible intuitions plays a fundamental role. Sensible intuition for Husserl is perception, and perception, as an act of consciousness, must have an object. In smelling, *something* is smelled; in hearing, something is heard, and in seeing, something is seen. Staying within the philosophical tradition in considering perception, Husserl gives vision, seeing, a certain priority by having it serve as the epitome of perception in general. Let us consider an example of visual perception from the phenomenological standpoint.

I see a tree. In what way, in what sense is this object given in the perceptual act of consciousness? It is not given as a representation; it is given as an *embodied presence*. Husserl embraces this notion of embodied presence in order to distinguish his from other theories of perception in which the object of perception is given as present in the status of a sign or symbol. Also, the object of perception is immediately given as present "bodily" in contrast to the modifications of "hovering before the mind" or being presented in memory or free fancy.[5] The tree, as the object of this perception, also falls under the category of "thing," as does every object of a perceptual act of consciousness.

The way in which the thing is given is also important; the thing, the object of sensory perception is given in a series of profiles, it is adumbrated. And this series of profiles is in principle infinite. That is, it is the very nature of the thing that it be given non-exhaustively. I cannot see both the back and the front of the tree at one and the same time, but the presence of

4 *Ibid.*, p. 55.
5 *Ibid.*, p. 136.

the front implicates the back; from the front which I see, the whole series of possible appearances is announced, implicated.

It is the very nature of any spatio-temporal object in reality to be given, to be perceived in this adumbrative manner.[6] This does not mean, however, that it is a mere sign or index which is perceived and that somehow the true imperceptible thing is merely indicated or signified by the series of appearances. The thing is not represented through its appearances; these appearances are aspects of the thing itself. We can see that here Husserl, in keeping with positivism, departs from Kant. For Kant the appearances were mere signs for the thing itself which could not be perceived, something which is other than, of a different level of being than, the sign which indicates it. For Husserl the appearance is not a *sign* for the thing; it is an aspect of it. It does not *indicate* the thing; it implicates the thing because it itself is a profile of the thing.

A sign and copy does not "announce" in itself the self that is signified (or copied). But the physical thing is nothing foreign to that which appears in a sensory body, but something that manifests itself in it and in it *alone*. Indeed in a primordial way, a way that is also *a priori* in that it rests on essential grounds something which cannot be annulled.[7]

In sensory perception what is perceived is the thing as present, manifested in bodily presence, not as a sign or symbol, but as itself, a concrete individual.[8] The thing is given to sensory perception through, or across, its profiles, given as a possible infinite series to a consciousness which perceives it. The mode in which the thing presents itself is in its bodily self-presence (*leibhaftigen Gegenwart*). Sensory perception is therefore an original mode of experience upon which other experiencing acts build as upon a ground. Perception has been established as a mode of experience, specifically a type of intuition in which the object is given in its bodily self-presence to a consciousness which intuits it as it is, directly given in sensory perception. It is in this sense that phenomenology can be considered as the doctrine that holds that seeing is believing.

It is on this point that phenomenology finds itself in opposition

[6] *Ibid.*, p. 134.
[7] *Ibid.*, p. 160.
[8] *Ibid.*, p. 76.

to scepticism and that empiricism which has its roots in scepticism. Scepticism in general is the position that all knowledge is uncertain, and its roots lie in the existence of perceptual illusion as a phenomenon. That is, scepticism holds that it is naive to "believe what is seen," since it is often self-evidently the case from experience that what one thought one saw was not in fact what one saw. The attack of scepticism then is that phenomenology claims a "bodily self-presence" for an object which is possibly only an illusury object, the object of sensory perception. Scepticism thereby maintains that there is an incompatibility in the notion that one and the same object can be claimed as both being present "bodily" and being only an illusury presence.

In order to justify his claim that the object of sensory perception has "bodily presence" it is incumbent upon Husserl to undermine the sceptic's position. Husserl ignores most of the classical arguments against scepticism and presents rather the argument that the sceptic sets up a false dilemma. He accomplishes this by showing that there is nothing incongruent in the notions of bodily presence and the possibility of illusion, as is claimed by the sceptic.

Husserl does not take up the position of Descartes who resolves, or rather dissolves, the problem of illusion by making it into a problem of judgemental activity. According to Descartes, it is not our senses which deceive us since in fact our perceptions are accurate enough; it is just that sometimes we "judge" too quickly about our perceptions. This means that the error involved in illusion lies on the level of judgement rather than on the level of perception. Illusion is here reduced to improper synthetic activity carried out by the faculty of judgement. Husserl cannot and does not use this method of escaping the dilemma; perception is indeed a synthetic act, but it is an act on the pre-judicative level. The synthesis involved in perception is not a matter of judging, but one of perceiving.

Resorting to the faculty of judgment as the source of error in the perceptual process, as did Descartes, is ultimately unintelligible. On what grounds can one judge that the previous judgment had been incorrect? Certainly not on the grounds of the object as perceived, since the original error was not perceptual. Where then does the second judgment derive its authority to correct the first? It is unsatisfactory to rely upon a concordance theory of truth, since that criterion would be purely on the level of judgments, whereas the perceptual activity is concerned with the immediate givenness of the object. By using previous judgments as the criteria of the real and the true the object itself is neglected and the original claim that the error is in judgment and not in perception is meaningless since the object plays no role in this criteria. It is only in an appeal to the object of perception that such a corrective judgment would be feasible. But for Descartes such a perception is impossible since it would necessarily have the same *perceptual* status as the first, which was also correct.

Husserl challenges the sceptics on their most primary assumption: that the source of illusion is the fallibility of the perceiving act alone which fails to perceive properly the object which is simply there, complete, just waiting to be properly perceived. It is this notion of the object as simply *there* which Husserl attacks. It is indeed there, in its bodily presence, but for a perceptual object to be there means, as Husserl has shown, to be there *as a series of appearances which are perceived in a series*. The object is not given all at once, but through or across this series of appearances. And this object of consciousness is not synthesized by either the object or by judgmental activity, but by the perceiving consciousness.[9] It is precisely because of the nature of the object, the thing, that illusion is possible. Since the thing is in principle never adequately perceived, not because of faulty perception but because of the nature of the thing, there is revealed a presupposition made by scepticism. Scepticism has always first taken for granted what it then makes dubious – the thing as necessarily existing as an absolute and therefore as knowable in itself. With the insight that it is the very nature of the thing to be given to consciousness perspectively (non-absolutely) the onus of being the only possible source of illusion is lifted from the perceiving consciousness.

One can now answer the question of how an illusion can be known to be an illusion, a knowledge which was inexplicable under scepticism. The object, itself being always in principle an infinite series of possible appearances to a perceiving consciousness, is now

[9] *Ibid.*, p. 334.

itself the force which reveals that an illusion has occurred. It reveals this illusion by "correcting" it through further adumbrations across or through which it is revealed more fully, more completely. The object in its bodily self-presence serves as the criterion by which an illusion as such can be perceptually recognized as having occurred. It was always this difficulty which was ultimately unaccounted for in the classical teaching of scepticism which placed the source of illusion as necessarily in the subjective rather than the objective pole of experience. Since it was presupposed that it was the nature of the object in itself to be given all at once, how could *it* be declared an illusion? Certainly not by a second perception of the object. Since the source of illusion was the perceiving activity, how could one choose between two perceptions and say that one was true and one an illusion? For an illusion to be recognized as such, it must be in contrast with a "proper" perception. But even if two distinct perceptions of the same object were different, how could one say which was true and which the illusion? And if, as the sceptics would have it, all sensory perceptions were illusory, how could one possibly know that? If there are no true perceptions, it is impossible to claim that perceptions are illusions, since illusion has meaning only in contrast with the true.

It is only through Husserl's insight which locates the source of the possibility of illusion in the very nature of the object itself, and thereby gives the object itself as the authority by which an illusion can be recognized as such, that illusion can be accounted for at all. And in this account the sceptical position in regard to sensory perceptual knowledge is demolished.

In summary we see that what is unique is that this teaching carries out the intent of radical empiricism more thoroughly than the teaching of the empiricists themselves. In regard to the object of sensory perception, Husserl demands *epistemological presence*; the object is given to the perceiving consciousness immediately and as it is. Sensory perception is understood as the primary mode of cognition of objects (things), and one which is fundamental in two senses. There is no higher faculty that can be appealed to to give a more "true" cognition of the thing, and there is no "unknown X" that is more real than that which appears by and across its series of appearances. What is known through sensory perception without mediation is real, and the sensible thing is really known through sensory perception. This is positivism in its richest sense. We shall now see how this positivism is carried over to the realm of essences as well as to that of facts.

D. FACT AND ESSENCE

In the first chapter of *Ideas* Husserl summarizes and carries over his work from the *Logische Untersuchungen* that has bearing on the logical background or foundation of phenomenology. These "logical considerations" as he calls them, revolve around the relation of fact and essence and the type of science that is proper to each, as well as the science proper to the relation of the two. Understanding this relation is vital in the thought of Husserl.

In accord with the empiricist understanding of science Husserl maintains that the natural sciences, the sciences of nature, are sciences of fact. That is, the empiricial sciences deal with facts, individuals within the realm of nature, as the subject matter of their respective sciences. For this reason, says Husserl, we can make the identification of the sciences of fact and the sciences of experience (*Erfahrung*).[10] This means that the ultimate ground of justification of such sciences lie in experience, which is to say, empirical intuition. There is, however, also another type of science, that which deals with the nonempirical as its subject matter. Sciences of this type are pure logic, pure time theory, pure mathematics, etc. Geometry has always been taken to be the epitome of this type of science, and Husserl concurs. From this difference in types of science Husserl presents an original doctrine concerning the nature of science as such, the relation of fact and essence, and the relation of the sciences which relate to each and the manner of that relation.

We have seen that the ultimate ground and justification for the empirical sciences is to be found in empirical intuition. This is clearly not the case for this second type of science. The reason for this is simply that the subject matter, the content of this second type of science, is not obtained from nor grounded in experience. This is crucial to the thinking of Husserl when he says:

[10] *Ibid.*, p. 51.

These, in all their thought-constructions, are free throughout from all positings of actual fact; or what comes to the same thing, *in them no experience qua experience*, i.e., *qua* consciousness that apprehends or sets up reality or concrete being, *can take over the function of supplying a logical ground*. Where experience functions in them, it is not *as* experience.[11]

Let us take geometry as our example for the clarification of this second type of science. It is immediately clear that the subject matter of geometry has nothing to do with the collection of factual data which can then be generalized in accordance with the laws of logic in order that it can become a science. The spatial relations which are the subject matter of Euclidean geometry are necessarily nonempirical since the best that one can hope to do is to reproduce on a blackboard with chalk rough approximations of the figures which are exactly determined by the axioms of geometry. These axioms are not contingent, and are necessarily determined independently of any experience of such figures in time and space. The relations among the angles of a triangle, that they must add up to 180 degress, are necessary ones and can be stated apodictically, contrary to the relations considered in the sciences of fact which are of the class of empirical generalizations. This necessity is determined by the essence of what it means to be a triangle, and it is here that we must locate the source that supplies the ultimate ground and justification for the sciences of the *a priori*, just as empirical intuition serves as the ultimate founding of the empirical sciences. *It is essential intuition*, essential insight, that is the source for the absolute grounding of these sciences. As Husserl says,

But for the geometer, who studies not actualities, but "ideal possibilities," not actual but essential relationships, *essential* insight and not experience is the act that supplies the ultimate grounds.[12]

We can see now why it is that Husserl calls these sciences we have been referring to as the *"a priori* sciences": *sciences of the essence*. The subject matters of these sciences are essences, and what supplies the fundamental ground for these sciences is the *intuition* of essences, just as, in an exactly parallel manner, the empirical sciences are given their grounding in empirical intuition. This is the first step in the original understanding which

[11] *Ibid.*, pp. 61–2.
[12] *Ibid.*, p. 62.

Husserl brings to bear concerning the epistemological and ontological ground of science, and it is here that he breaks with the
traditional empiricist concept of science.

For Husserl, essential insight is always no less possible than
individual intuition. It is here that he goes beyond classical
empiricism, for which essences were not accessible through intuition whatever their metaphysical status might be. The grounds
upon which Husserl justifies this insistence on the philosophical
legitimacy of essences are twofold: logical considerations as noted
above, and, what is more important for us, epistemological
grounds. Through the process of *ideation* the epistemological and
ontological status of essences is understood by Husserl as showing
that essences are the *objects of certain primary dator intuitions*. He
says:

> At first "essence" indicated that which in the ultimate self-being of an
> individual discloses to us "what" it is. But every such what can be "set
> out as an idea." *Empirical or individual intuition* can be transformed into
> *essential insight* (ideation) – a possibility which is itself not to be under-
> stood as empirical but as essential possibility. The object of such insight is
> then the corresponding *pure* essence or eidos, whether it be the highest
> category or one of its specializations, right down to the fully "concrete."[13]

This notion that essences are the objects of certain primary
dator intuitions is the ultimate fundamental ground for the justification of the existence of any object whatsoever. This means
that it is precisely on the same grounds that empiricism generally
operates in the epistemological justification of science in general
and the determination of validity of judgments as empirically
verifiable, that Husserl carries through his teaching concerning
essences and the science of essences. As primary dator intuitions
which are given in a way exactly parallel to empirical primary
dator intuitions, the intuition of essences supplies the ultimate
grounds for discourse about those individuals. To be sure, the
intuitions are only parallel and not the same; they differ in
principle. This can be seen in considering the relationship which
exists between the two types of sciences that have as their ultimate foundations these two types of intuitions.

It is imperative to understand here that what Husserl is pro-
posing is not merely the idea that the empiricists' notion of science
was incomplete and that it was all right as far as it went. This is

[13] *Ibid.*, p. 54.

exactly what would be the case if Husserl merely maintained that there exist sciences of the essence which, just like sciences of fact, have their grounding in corresponding intuitions, and that the classical empiricists in their rigor overlooked the intuition of essences, an oversight that we have now corrected. But if Husserl is correct about the sciences of the essence, then there also follows a new understanding of the sciences of fact, for Husserl *insists* upon the *interdependence* of the sciences of the fact and the sciences of the essence. He reveals a new dimension of the old slogan that from facts follow nothing but facts. He shows that the very notion of any science at all would be totally incomprehensible if one denies the efficacy of essences, as the positivists do.[14] In the first place, every empirical science uses a system of reasoning, that is, a system of mediation to make scientific judgments, and this *scientific reasoning* proceeds according to the principles of formal logic, and formal logic is a science of the essence, not of the emprical. Secondly, in order to be a science at all every science must be directed at *objects*, and objects of a special type within an ontological region, that region of being with which the science deals. The cognition and articulation of ontological regions and objects are determined by the "laws which pertain to the essence of objectivity in general."[15] Objectivity as such then, and as necessary to science in general, is the object of eidetic science, not empirical science. As Husserl says, "Every factual science (empirical science) has essential theoretical bases in eidetic ontologies."[16]

There exists then a clear and necessary interdependence between the two types of sciences. But it is important to realize that this interdependence is strictly one-directional; the empirical sciences depend upon the eidetic sciences in order to be science, but the reverse is not the case. The sciences of the essence, which include all *a priori* sciences, are logically, ontologically, and as we shall see, epistemologically prior.[17] This relationship of the two types of science is not contingent; it is necessary. This necessity is revealed by considering the relation between fact and essence, and most particularly by the difference in principle between the intuition of facts and the intuition of essence.

[14] *Ibid.*, pp. 62–3.
[15] *Ibid.*, p. 63.
[16] *Ibid.*, p. 64.
[17] *Ibid.*, pp. 77–8.

Let us not miss what lies at the heart of this unique doctrine of Husserl – *that there is intuition of essences*, and that these intuitions can have the status of a *primordial dator act*. This means that Husserl does not limit himself to merely carrying through those insights accepted by the classical empiricists (as for example in the case of his rejection of the Kantian teaching of the thing-in-itself as somehow behind the appearances on positivist principles). He is radical precisely because he extends the field of the applicability of the positivist doctrine to areas declared explicitly illegitimate by the empiricists themselves. And he makes this claim not in the name of idealism (although that too is involved), nor in the name of Platonic realism, but in the name of positivism.

If by "Positivism" we are to mean the absolute unbiased grounding of all science on what is "positive," i.e., on what can be primordially apprehended, then it is *we* who are the genuine positivists.[18]

It is from the existence of the sciences of the essence that Husserl argues for the acceptance of the notion that there is a type of intuition which, in a manner parallel to empirical intuition and empirical objects, grasps, receives in a primordial way, this object, the *eidos*. Husserl defines this briefly:

At first "essence" indicated that which in the intimate self-being of an individual discloses to us "what it is." But every such What can be "set out as an idea."[19]

This object, which Husserl identifies as the *eidos*, is the object of an act of consciousness. These are certain terminological clarifications that need to be made at this point, specifically the meanings of the terms "experience" and "intuition."

The possibility of cognitions of no matter what order or type is possible only within the realm of consciousness, and because consciousness is always consciousness of .... Epistemologically speaking then, consciousness is the absolute condition for the possibility of knowledge. Not all acts of consciousness are the same, however. As does Kant, Husserl defines the world as "the totality of objects that can be known through experience (*Erfah-*

---

[18] *Ibid.*, p. 86.
[19] *Ibid.*, p. 54.

rung)."[20] This is a definition with an epistemological purpose, but it of course involves a certain ontological thesis concerning the world and objects, if only implicitly. What is important, however, is that the world is *not* defined as the totality of all objects whatsoever. Husserl grants that there are other types of objects, and as a corollary, that there are other modes of knowledge than that which knows wordly objects. That is, these other objects are the objects of modes of consciousness other than what has traditionally been known as experience. It is for this reason that Husserl uses the wider term intuition,[21] to indicate modes of cognition which bring objects of whatever type into presence. Experience therefore refers to one type and one realm of intuition, that which has as its objects "wordly" objects. Another type and realm of intuition is *Erlebnis*, which can also be translated as "experience." An *Erlebnis* has as its object something which is of the same order in the stream of consciousness itself. *Erlebnisse* are then of the realm of what is usually called "inner experience," although Husserl does not like that term. After further development we shall be able to refer to immanent experiences and the transcendental realm.[22]

In the *Logische Untersuchungen* Husserl used the term *ideation* to refer to that cognitive process which is called the *Wesenschau*, essential insight or eidetic intuition in the *Ideas*. He abandons the former term for the latter because he feels that a more "plastic" term is needed to fully comprehend the function that he wishes the term to express.[23] But the term "ideation" had an advantage which "essential intuition" and its variants do not; it emphasized that this intuition is achieved as a *process*. Ideation is the process which results in the intuition of an *eidos*, an essence. And, as we have already mentioned, it is an intuition that is parallel, as regards the respective objects, to empirical intuition. First let us see how the process of ideation is analogous to empirical intuition.

Husserl labors to show that ideation is not the process of abstraction and/or conceptualization in the usual sense of mental construct.[24] This means that ideation is *not* a process of mediation,

[20] *Ibid.*, p. 51.
[21] *Ibid.*, p. 85.
[22] *Ibid.*, pp. 137–14, 215–227, *et passim*.
[23] *Ibid.*, p. 56.
[24] *Ibid.*, pp. 89–90, 202–208.

a process in the sense of being a series of graduated steps or procedures which lead to or end up in a final step, the revelation of the *eidos*. In rejecting this concept of essence and the cognition of essence Husserl necessarily places himself directly within the philosophical tradition which we have named the metaphysics of presence. For it is significant that ideation is the *bringing to presence* of an object – the *eidos*.

All intuition has the function of making present; but what is remarkable is Husserl's claim that eidetic intuition, like sensory perception, can be *primordial* and not derivative. Imagination, for example, is a derivative mode of intuition; it too brings objects into presence, but its function is precisely *re*-presentation. It is a modified act of consciousness since it must derive its objects of imagination from prior acts of consciousness, like sensory perception. Modified acts of consciousness do not *give* their objects originally. Only primordial dator acts make present, bring into originating presence, their objects. It is this central factor which allows Husserl to conclude: "In particular essential insight is a primordial dator act, and as such analogous to sensory perception, and not to imagination." [25]

That ideation can be an original primordial dator intuition and yet come out of other, and even other non-primordial intuitions are explicable through the original Husserlean teaching concerning essence, and this brings out equally the key role which the notion of presence plays here. Ideation is the "shift of attention" which is a transformation of an empirical or individual intuition into an essential one. This transformation is the *making present* of a *new* object – the *eidos*. This object is not, and cannot be given by, an individual intuition. This means however, as Husserl points out, that the *eidos* is given primordially in ideation as the originating act of consciousness through which alone the object comes into presence. [26] If the insight is essential insight in the strong sense, a true "making present," a giving of the object, then it is a primordial dator act.

Every possible object, or to put it logically, "every subject of possibly true predications," has indeed *its own* ways, that of predicative thinking above all, of coming under a glance that presents, intuits, meets it even-

[25] *Ibid.*, p. 92.
[26] *Ibid.*, p. 55.

tually in its "bodily selfhood" and "lays hold of" it. Thus essential insight is intuition, and if it is insight in the pregnant sense of the term, and not a mere, and possibly vague, representation, it is a *primordial* dator intuition, grasping the essence in its "bodily" selfhood.[27]

This bringing to presence (in the strong sense) is what makes essential intuition parallel to empirical intuition; ideation strives to bring to presence through the medium of an *individual* counterpart or illustration of the essence. Like empirical individual intuition, therefore, it brings its object – the essence – to visibility and gives it in "bodily selfhood."[28] Ideation is a *spontaneous* process – but it is not the object, but rather the *consciousness of the object* that is engendered in the spontaneous act. And ideation is necessarily spontaneous – one is necessarily busied with the apprehended object since this is the only way that the object can be brought into presence. Ideation is this bringing into presence, this being "busied," taken up, with the presence of the object. Ideation is the presentation of the essence.[29]

Already here a difference in principle, that is, an essential difference, between essential intuition and empirical intuition is manifest. Spontaneity, although possible, is not necessary to empirical consciousness in the giving of sensory objects. There is, for example, marginal awareness and other modifications of this type.[30] But along with this difference comes the single great difference which breaks the analogy between empirical intuition and essential intuition. Despite the fact that it too is the striving to bring into visible presence of its object, the fact remains that eidetic intuition is not dependent upon individual empirical intuition. Empirical intuition is concerned with *existence* (in the sense of individual concrete being) and has as its "goal" the making present of such an object, of positing it as existing. The making present through an intuition of the essence is precisely the bringing into presence of an essence, of which it must be possible that there is a counterpart or illustration, but which in no way involves the positing of that exemplar as a concrete, existing, individual being. The essence does not exist as an *individual* being, since it is precisely the essence of essence to be other than con-

[27] *Ibid.*, pp. 55–6.
[28] *Ibid.*, p. 56.
[29] *Ibid.*, p. 91.
[30] *Ibid.*, pp. 265–270.

crete individual *Dasein*. This essential difference in the intuition of essence and empirical intuition is exactly that of the difference between *fact* and *eidos*.[31]

This is sustained by the fact that the starting point of ideation is not necessarily (in the strong sense of the term) an empirical, real, intuition. It can serve equally well, and in most instances serve the purpose better, to set out from intuitions of the imagination, which in no sense posit existence. Husserl refers to the privileged role of fantasy in phenomenology as a way to the essence.[32] Setting out from non-real, nonexisting-positing intuitions does not, however, prevent *primordial dator intuitions* even though they are not themselves primordial.

Hence, with the aim of grasping an essence itself in its primordial form we can set out from corresponding empirical intuitions, but we can also set out just as well from non-empirical intuitions, intuitions that do not apprehend sensory existence, intuitions rather "of a merely imaginary order."[33]

Essences therefore and their intuitions are independent of facts and their intuitions since they need not be based on fact. Ideation is the bringing to presence of essences, but makes no assertion of existence within the realm of the empirical.

In summary, then, we can see that Husserl reverses the empiricists' conclusion concerning the status of essences by bringing to bear the most fundamental criteria and underlying theses of all of positivism: that the fundamental dimensions of knowledge must be *primordial dator acts*. And although empirical intuition and essential insight differ in principle because of the type of being attributable to their respective objects, as is made manifest in the consideration we have offered of the play of fancy as a source of intuitions of essences, nonetheless the two types of intuition, the cognitive processes, are parallel precisely insofar as they have the same "goal" and provide the same sort of "justification" for their respective objects. The nature of any act of ideation involves the bringing into visible presence of its object, just as the nature of sensory perception involves the bringing into visible presence of the sensory object. Each of these object-giving

[31] *Ibid.*, p. 56.
[32] *Ibid.*, pp. 198–99.
[33] *Ibid.*, p. 57.

intuitions can be primordial dator intuitions, the fundamental justification and grounding of any cognition whatsoever.

This, then, constitutes the fundamental part of our claim that Husserl carries through the intent of what we call the metaphysics of presence, this positing of primordial immediate intuition as the movement that gives knowledge of being through presence. But it is clear that not all knowledge is of the type of direct intuition. And further, not every intuition can qualify as being what Husserl calls a primordial dator act. Husserl sees this perfectly well; there is "founded" knowledge, as well as non-primordial intuition. But part of the task of phenomenology according to Husserl is to carry out an intentional analysis on all types of founded knowledge to discover the founding intuitions, the primordial dator intuitions which are the only absolute source of authority for knowledge. Husserl must make this claim that it is possible in principle to arrive, through intentional analysis, at the founding intuitions of knowledge. If this claim were not made and carried through, it would be possible to interpret this epistemology as leaving open the possibility that knowledge could be founded through non-presence, that is, by a non-presence of consciousness to its intentional object. This possibility would be in direct contradiction to the deepest effort of Husserl himself to rejoin and revitalize that thought which we have referred to as the metaphysics of presence. At this point we must follow out Husserl's thought that non-presence can and must be reduced to some more primordial presence which is given in an epistemologically absolute sense, and that it is upon this that the knowledge of the absent can be founded.

E. PHENOMENOLOGY AS SCIENCE

We have already examined the relationship of the sciences of fact and the sciences of the essence. What now is the relation that exists with these sciences and phenomenology? Phenomenology is an eidetic science, and it serves as a foundation and grounding of the sciences of fact.[34] Phenomenology, however, is also a science that serves as a foundation and grounding for the sciences of the essence as well. And finally, phenomenology is the science that

---

[34] *Ibid.*, p. 201, *et passim.*

provides its own grounding; that serves as its own foundation.[35] This unique quality allows Husserl to declare phenomenology to be "First Philosophy," emphasizing the position of this science as the grounding science and branch of philosophy upon which all of the other branches of knowledge ultimately rest.

What is it about phenomenology that allows it to "stand under" the other sciences, both of fact and essence? How is it that phenomenology is more fundamental and different than, say, geometry, rather than being a parallel science which has no essential connection with it? A first answer is that it is the science which allows for the systematic articulation of the real distinction between the sciences of fact and the sciences of the essence. Of course this distinction was noted before Husserl; but it is Husserl's contention that where this articulation took place it was done and could only have been done from the unrecognized perspective of a First Philosophy. Husserl does not claim to invent phenomenology *ex nihilo*; he himself refers to the work of Descartes, Locke, Hume and Kant on this point.[36] But they did not realize the import of their own insights in this regard and allowed the grasp they had on phenomenology to escape them. They did not realize that in their efforts at first philosophy they had come upon a different region of being – the region of pure consciousness.

The sciences of fact are sciences about the world; the subject matter with which they deal are entities and processes which occur in the "natural world." But as Husserl points out this in itself makes a certain demand about the type of relationship of attitude and perspectival standpoint that scientists can have with the objects of their science. It involves both the "thesis of the natural standpoint" and the dogmatic attitude.

The dogmatic attitude of which Husserl speaks is not to be understood in a derogatory sense at all; it is the simple affirmation that scientists (not only in the natural sciences) operate dogmatically in the sense that they do not raise epistemological questions, nor do they attend to the theoretical philosophical problems that might relate to their field of enquiry.[37] Included among that which is "overlooked," for example, are those neces-

---

[35] *Ibid.*, pp. 182, 187-9.
[36] *Ibid.*, p. 183.
[37] *Ibid.*, pp. 95-7.

sary insights, perhaps of a methodological character, that come from those eidetic sciences like logic, but which the scientist feels constrained to declare to be metaphysical ghosts on the theoretical basis of "positivism."[38] Biologists, for example, in pursuing their work in the laboratory, do not ask how is biology possible, nor what type of ontological status the being which is studied by biology has, but rather raise only those questions and carry through those methods which are part of the biological science itself. Dogmatics here is to be understood then in the sense that the working scientist takes the facts that are given, and takes them as such, and applies to them only the methods and questions that flow directly from the very nature of the science.

The dogmatic attitude in the sciences is a specialized instance of what Husserl calls the "general thesis of the natural standpoint."[39] This "thesis" is the manner and original mode in which we encounter and deal with the world, or how we know it. The real world is apprehended as a world of facts, that is, as a world that has its *being out there*.[40] This is the general thesis of the natural standpoint. As a thesis, however, it is not an act in the usual sense; it is not an articulated existential judgment. It is rather the *ground* for all judgments of fact, or existence, or about the world in general. It functions in every questioning of the factual givenness of, or in, the world.

> This "fact world," as the word already tells us, I find to be out there, and also take it just as it gives itself to me as something that exists out there. All doubting and rejecting of the data of the natural world leaves standing the general thesis of the natural standpoint.[41]

The sciences of nature all operate within this natural standpoint in order to know the world more perfectly and completely than naive experience allows.[42] This is of course not the only way of relating to the world; *all* the relations I have with the world are grounded in the natural standpoint. I find myself a part of this world around me. The fundamental form in which I live my waking life and relate to the world and its contents is announced in the Cartesian expression: *Cogito*. Like Descartes, Husserl includes in

---

[38] *Ibid.*, p. 93.
[39] *Ibid.*, pp. 105–6.
[40] *Ibid.*, p. 107.
[41] *Ibid.*, p. 106.
[42] *Ibid.*

the expression *cogito* all of the various modes of consciousness: thinking, perceiving, wishing, willing, recollecting, etc.[43] Every *cogito* has its object, its *cogitatum*, thereby manifesting the intentional nature of consciousness. And it is clear that not every *cogitatum* need be of the sensory field of objects; the *cogito* itself can become an object of reflection, of remembering, in short, an object of a new *cogito*. Also, of course, the cogito need not be concerned with facts of the fact-world; I can just as well take an "arithmetical standpoint" which makes the arithmetical world that which concerns me. But even when I am not occupied with the fact-world, the natural standpoint is operative.

Perhaps I am busied with pure numbers and the laws they symbolize; nothing of this sort is present in the world about me, this world of "real fact" ... The arithmetical world is there for me only when and so long as I occupy the arithmetical standpoint. But the natural world, the world in the ordinary sense of the word, is constantly there for me, so long as I live naturally and look in its direction. ... The natural world still remains "present," I am at the natural standpoint after as well as before, and in this respect undisturbed by the adoption of new standpoints.[44]

If this is the natural standpoint, how is it that it is referred to as a "thesis" at all, since every thesis must in principle be capable of not being posited? It shows itself to be a thesis in that, if it cannot be contradicted, it can be disconnected, bracketed, and replaced and modified by another standpoint, that of scepticism, for example, or the universal doubt of Descartes. Since in order for it to be possible to doubt the being of this or that, or of a whole realm of being as does Descartes, it must therefore be possible to put out of action the thesis which affirms that being and to take another standpoint. There is possible the *suspension* of every thesis, the natural standpoint no less than any other. All theses could fall under an *epoché*; in this sense it is parallel to Descartes' universal doubt. But we do not wish to carry through a doubt, rather to bring about the suspension of a certain thesis. This means that we are not performing a total epoché, we are not engaged in suspending all possible theses; nor are we *denying* the thesis of the natural standpoint. This thesis which supports experience of a certain type of being of the natural world as self-evidently given, and which supports those sciences which operate from within this

[43] *Ibid.*, p. 104.
[44] *Ibid.*

standpoint and the validity of whose judgments concerning the entities of the world we do not question, is merely suspended. It is this and only this which we bracket, and we do so self-consciously. That means that we can now still deal with this same world, but only with the qualification that it is bracketed, that these existential judgments of the sciences are no longer operable. This limited form of the epoché is the phenomenological epoché.

> We put out of action the general thesis which belongs to the essence of the natural standpoint, we place in brackets whatever it includes respecting the nature of Being: this entire natural world therefore which is continually "there" for us "present to our hand," and will ever remain there, is a "fact world" of which we continue to be conscious, even though it pleases us to put it in brackets.
>
> If I do this, as I am fully free to do, I do not then deny this "world" as though I were a sophist, I do not doubt that it is there as though I were a sceptic; but I use the "phenomenological" epoché, which completely bars me from using any judgment that concerns spatio-temporal existence (*Dasein*).[45]

We see then what are the results of the phenomenological epoché in a negative sense, the effect it has of suspending judgments concerning the being of the world. But what is of primary importance is the positive effect. By means of the bracketing a *new region of being has been revealed*, one which is complete in its own right, and totally accessible to consciousness. That region is nothing other than consciousness itself. It is this which first of all sets apart phenomenology from the other eidetic sciences; the whole region of consciousness is the object of the science of phenomenology. Since the other eidetic sciences all deal with species of objects of consciousness (the highest genus of which is consciousness), the science of consciousness is the one that can serve as the grounding ontology for all of the sciences of this sphere.

> Consciousness in itself has a being of its own which in its absolute uniqueness of nature remains unaffected by the phenomenological disconnection. It therefore remains over as a "phenomenological residuum," as a region of Being which is in principle unique, and can become in fact the field of a new science – the science of Phenomenology.[46]

The phenomenological epoché, combined with that process which Husserl calls ideation, that shift to the consideration of

---

45 *Ibid.*, pp. 110–111.
46 *Ibid.*, p. 113.

essences which is in principle always possible, allows us now to see what is the reason of the science of phenomenology: it is the science of the essences of consciousness.

The Being of Consciousness

Let us see exactly what it is that has been accomplished by means of the epoché in the broadest epistemological terms. The world of our everyday experience is that which is encountered in the thesis of the natural standpoint, and it is this standpoint which falls with the institution of the phenomenological epoché. What status does the world now have? For Husserl as for Kant, the things of the world are essentially other than that which appears as being within the stream of consciousness itself, in that they have the character of being transcendent. For Kant this means that the appearances of the world had the quality of being appearances of things-in-themselves which were themselves in principle unknowable, and the world therefore was experienced as a phenomenal world, behind which existed, in some unknown sense, the things. The world has been reduced to mere phenomena.

The world according to Husserl is also phenomena, but in a sense radically different from that of Kant. By means of the phenomenological epoché, the appearances of the world are maintained as what they were before, with the modification that it appears as *meant*, as correlate of the acts of consciousness. However, for Husserl this does not in the least imply that they do not really exist, or that the transcendent things exist as some unknowable X. The purpose of the epoché most clearly shows itself here. The validity of propositions concerning the world no longer depend upon positing the existence of the things in a form either knowable or unknowable, for precisely that suspension of the thesis concerning the factual character of the world (that is, positing it as existing) has been put out of play, and the validating criteria for judgments have become the *phenomena as they appear*, and nothing else. Of course, as has already been noted, there is a difference between experience transcendentally directed and experience immanently directed. But the criteria and source for this differentiation are to be found in consciousness itself. As Husserl shows, statements about transcendent being have their source in a specific act of consciousness which *gives* that being in a certain intuition, that of evidential vision, an immediate essential intuition.

> We must therefore not let ourselves be deceived by any talk about the transcendence of the thing over against consciousness or about its "Being-in-itself." The genuine concept of thing-transcendence which is the standard whereby all rational statements about transcendence are measured, cannot be extracted from any source other than the perception's own essential content, or the definitely articulated connections which we call evidential (*ausweisenden*) experience. The idea of this transcendence is thus the eidetic correlate of the pure idea of this evidential experience.[47]

In summary, then, we say that the world is still there for me, but it is there as a phenomenon which is given as meaningful as it appears to consciousness. If indeed a part of this meaning is its transcendent character as compared with the immanent character of the stream of consciousness itself, this is solely on the grounds of the appearing as such, and does not refer to anything beyond the being of the phenomenon. Husserl carries this theme through as strongly as possible by exercising a hypothetical annihilation of the world. Even if one thinks through the possibility of the non-being of every transcendent thing, the being of consciousness would not be annihilated, although modified.[48] No real thing is necessary for the being of consciousness itself. The sphere of consciousness therefore becomes for Husserl the transcendental sphere, and phenomenology becomes transcendental phenomenology.[49] This is a theme which is emphasized much more in the later works and which is presented very strongly in the preface to the English edition of *Ideas*.[50]

For our purposes the efficacy of the phenomenological epoché is twofold. (1) The world is understood as phenomenal being and is meaningful only in relation to consciousness.[51] (2) Consciousness, as the being that remains as residue after the institution of the reduction, is given as the absolute region of being that is given totally to consciousness itself.[52] Let us consider now how it is that being and presence are given as absolutely primordial within the transcendental sphere.

[47] *Ibid.*, p. 148.
[48] *Ibid.*, p. 151.
[49] *Ibid.*, p. 251.
[50] *Ibid.*, p. 11, *et passim*.
[51] *Ibid.*, p. 147.
[52] *Ibid.*, p. 154.

F. INTENTIONAL ANALYSIS

We have previously seen that the essence of consciousness is intentionality. It is only now, after we have performed the reduction to evoke the uniquely phenomenological sphere that we can follow out what is involved in this principle. Intentionality is the main phenomenological theme, and the intentional structure can be revealed through analysis; precisely this is the task of phenomenological description.[53]

Intentionality reveals itself as having two correlative poles, the noetic or subjective pole, and the noematic or objective pole. The noetic phase is that of the acts of consciousness, while the noematic is the object of consciousness. The object of consciousness is always a sense, a meaning, something intended, something meant, and the acts of consciousness are what make present this meaning.[54] All of this is to be understood as dealing with the essences involved, since phenomenology concerns itself with the *eidos*, not with the fact. Let it be noted, however, that although one-sided analyses are possible and sometimes even necessary, any truly phenomenological investigation and description must take into consideration the constitution of both the noetic and noematic poles, to be complete, since this involves the phenomenologically inseparable relation that is intentionality. The originating function of consciousness in relation to being has its source within this relationship. This allows Husserl to claim: "It is the original category of Being generally (or as we would put it, the original region), in which all other regions have their root." [55]

Let us consider a noema, say a woman once loved. This same noema, this woman once loved, can be brought to presence through several possible noetic acts or modifications of noetic acts. She can be seen on the street one day. Or, she can appear as an illusion, a play of fancy, when in fact it is really someone else whom I see. Or she can be remembered, or she can be the object of my judgment, or of my bad will. In short, every noema has its corresponding noesis in which it is presented as the meaning which is

[53] *Ibid.*, pp. 241–244.
[54] *Ibid.*, pp. 257 ff.
[55] *Ibid.*, p. 212.

meant. What unifies these experiences is the intentional relationship, and it is the structure of intentionality that justifies
the claim that they are the acts of one and the same stream of
consciousness.[56] On the noematic side we have a meaning, a sense,
an essence (*Sinn*) that is the same in all modifications in which it
is presented. All of the ways in which it is presented are modes of
intuition or their modifications. But Husserl's remarkable teaching is that not all modes of intuition have the same epistemological
status; that a type of hierarchy exists in the essential relationships that hold among the different modes and modifications of
intuitions.

As we have seen previously from the "principle of principles,"
the absolute criterion of validity of knowledge resides in primordial dator acts of consciousness. Now Husserl shows us that it is
possible in principle, through intentional analysis, to "trace back"
all modifications of the original modes of consciousness to those
originary modes.[57] This assures the same degree of validity for
the modifications as for those original intuitions which were the
bringing of the object into presence.

> Conversely, starting from any experience which has already the char-
> acter of such a modification, and remains then always so characterized *in
> itself*, we are lead back to certain original experiences, to impressions
> which exhibit experiences that in the phenomenological sense are abso-
> lutely primordial.[58]

We shall take up the process by which this occurs and is understood in more detail in the next chapter. What needs to be
clarified now is the general epistemological and ontological meaning of what has been worked out here.

It is as the result of the phenomenological epoché that there is
won the sphere of transcendental consciousness itself. This reduction has two epistemological effects in regard to the bringing
into presence of being. On the one hand, there is the fact of the
reduction itself, which gives to consciousness that one region of
being which is absolutely accessible to consciousness, and which
allows consciousness to disintegrate opacity between itself and its

[56] *Ibid.*, p. 242.
[57] *Ibid.*, p. 413.
[58] *Ibid.*, p. 221.

object. And this region is the original region, the region upon which all others depend. Secondly, this allows that all of the modes of consciousness can now be understood as modifications of consciousness of the primordial dator intuitions, those through which being is self-evidently given. This means that in principle it is possible to return to that absolute evidence, that *presence to being* in which the object, given to consciousness in its originary mode as bodily presence, has an indubitable claim to being.

It is in this way that Husserl elaborates an epistemology in which the primordial bodily presence of an object is the only meaningful criterion of knowledge, including metaphysical knowledge. And according to Husserl, phenomenology's work as an epistemology is to comprehend being in a positive sense and set, through its understanding, the foundations for positive science of all kinds. This is to be done through the accessibility phenomenology has to the region that is for Husserl the sphere of absolute being, where consciousness achieves unmediated presence to absolute being.

We have seen that there are several epistemological levels where the movement toward presence occurs. There is first of all the presence of facts, concrete individual objects. By his destruction of the sceptical position on perception, Husserl restores the object of perception to a condition of being present. In regard to the "presence of facts," presence means that the object itself is given in immediate intuition, and given as it is. It is given in profiles because that is the mode of givenness appropriate to the *being* of the object. The individual object is given in empirical intuition, and it is given as a bodily presence. It is not a representation, nor a sign, but an immediate bodily presence. As revealed in immediate intuition, these objects manifest being. Facts are given as an unimpeachable source of knowledge of what is. This is in keeping with the doctrine of the metaphysics of presence.

Husserl's most radical step, we have said, is the extension of positivism to the realm of essences. He holds that eidetic intuition is directly parallel to empirical intuition since ideation brings the object to presence. The presence of the eidos to consciousness serves as the foundation of eidetic knowledge and the foundation of eidetic science, since primordial dator intuitions function as *evidence* in any system of knowledge, whether empirical or eidetic.

The evidential vision is the epistemological moment in the Husserlean teaching, and it is this that is so laboriously worked through in *Ideas*, and then taken up again and again in his work. But this theme is no less the guiding intuition of that line of Western thought that we call the metaphysics of presence. It is within Husserl's doctrine of language that we discover the further articulation of the theory of *Evidenz*.

CHAPTER III

TRUTH AND PRESENCE

There are three main reasons why we shall take up the question
of language at this point in our study.

First, the question of language in general is at the heart of any
philosophical endeavor whether it is explicitly dealt with or not,
since philosophy attempts to say something, to speak about what
is. And what is said is said through language. This raises for any
philosophical effort the fundamental question of the relation of
speaking to what is spoken about. That is, the relation between
the being of language and the language of being. This is particularly true of phenomenology since as Husserl conceives it, it is a
descriptive science. The question of language is important to
phenomenology in a double sense; because it explicitly claims to
be descriptive, and because it claims to be a science. Description
is a linguistic act, and science is objectified in the medium of
expression, i.e., language.[1]

Secondly, Husserl himself began the self-conscious development
of phenomenology in the investigation of language. It is in an
effort to solve specific problems concerning the nature of logic
(of which language is a central element for Husserl) that Husserl
out of necessity begins to develop phenomenology. The question
and problems which are at the heart of phenomenology – the
concepts of intentionality, evidence, eidetic intuition, the relation
meaning-meant, etc. – are first encountered in this consideration
of language. Furthermore, it is the case that to a large extent
these concepts, as they are developed and unfolded in the consideration of language, are then taken as the models or archetypes
when they are involved in the investigation of non-linguistic
phenomena. This is particularly true of the concept of intention-

[1] Husserl, *Ideas*, p. 348.

ality. It therefore behooves us to have this original understanding of the concept which Husserl himself has, if we are to attempt to validly examine his doctrine concerning these concepts when they come up in relation to non-linguistic phenomena.

Finally, in undertaking this investigation of Husserl's teaching on language we shall see that it is permeated through and through by that line of thinking which we have called the metaphysics of presence. Husserl's adherence to this doctrine most clearly comes through first in his views on language. In the consideration of language the conformity of phenomenology and the metaphysics of presence first occurs, and therefore is first revealed.

Derrida takes this fact to mean that it is *because* of the adherence of the theory of signs to this doctrine that Husserl's other work becomes dependent upon the metaphysics of presence as well. But we contend that the theory of signs is itself not primordial, but rather rests upon an epistemological structure that supports it. *Beneath* the theory of signs is the teaching on evidence. As the results of our investigation, we shall bring out the following points:

1. That the concept of evidence is central to Husserl's understanding of language.

2. That the concept of evidence is in conformity with, and grows out of, the ideal of the metaphysics of presence that Husserl holds as the guiding notion of epistemology.

3. That out of the twofold relation of evidence with (a) language, and (b) perception at its limits, there arises a double understanding of the nature of consciousness: consciousness as interpretive act, and consciousness as representative act.

4. That consciousness understood as interpretation is arrived at by Husserl through his understanding of language as "signs interpreted to mean."

5. That on the other hand the notion of evidence requires the understanding of consciousness as a representative act. And this means that it is from his understanding of language that there necessarily results a dual understanding of consciousness.

6. That in fact Husserl's description of language is based upon an incomplete view of the phenomenon: the work of structural linguistics, particularly that of de Saussure, shows that in order to understand language as a system, it is necessary to see it in

terms of the tension resulting from the co-primordiality of absence and presence.

7. That it is not necessary to hold two different views of the nature of consciousness to understand language, since it is because of his views on language that Husserl developed these conceptions of consciousness.

A. EXPRESSION AND MEANING

The question of language is brought up only obliquely in *Ideas*, and then treated in an extremely concentrated form. (Sections 11, 124, 127, 134.) In fact, when it is brought up for the first time it is not considered a problem at all. Husserl says with confidence:

> We add here this further remark, that by "categories" we can understand, on the one hand, concepts in the sense of meanings but on the other also, and to better effect, the formal essences themselves which find their expression in these meanings. For instance, the "category" substantive meaning, plurality, and the like ultimately mean the formal eidos substantive meaning generally, plurality, and the like. The equivocation is dangerous only so long as one has not learned to separate clearly what must here be separated on all occasions: "meaning," and that which in virtue of its meaning permits of being expressed; and again: meaning and objectivity meant.[2]

Husserl feels quite confident that he has already treated of the problem of expression, i.e., language, in the *Logische Untersuchungen*, and he quite often refers the reader of *Ideas* to that work for further clarification of the matter. Thus we must return to that work if we are going to acquire an explicative understanding of Husserl's doctrine of language and the notions which underlie it.

This is a quite legitimate enterprise; it is in no way to pit an earlier doctrine against a later one. Husserl after the writing of *Ideas* returned and extensively reworked those sections of the *Logische Untersuchungen* which he felt needed such reworking to bring them into accord with the more sophisticated phenomenological research of the later work.[3] Husserl never repudiated this early work except to declare that it was not exhaustive and tended to attack problems in a one-sided manner. Our first

---

[2] *Ibid.*, pp. 68–9.
[3] Marvin Farber, *The Foundations of Phenomenology*, 3rd edition (Albany: The Research Foundation of The State University of New York, 1967), p. 199.

task is to see what is Husserl's teaching and how he arrived at it by examining it as it appears in the revised work of the *Logische Untersuchungen*.

In understanding Husserl's phenomenological research on language it is important to realize that he approaches it from the standpoint of what he has already worked out concerning the nature of logic in the first volume of the *Logische Untersuchungen* which is subtitled: *Prolegomena zur reinen Logik*. Meanings are for Husserl logical objects; that is, they are *ideal*. But these ideal objects are given in empirical grammatical forms. In short, ideal objects are expressed in concrete experience. For Husserl the problematic of language is therefore grounded in the question of how meaning is related to expression.[4]

Husserl begins his investigation with a consideration of the concept of signs (*Zeichen*). Every sign is a sign *of* something, but there is a distinction to be drawn between two types of signs. There is one type of sign which essentially is an indicator; it has the function of indicating something else, and the sign does not necessarily express a meaning. There is, however, also another type of sign, that which has or carries a sense or meaning which is expressed by the sign. The terms "expression" and "sign" therefore are not synonymous, and linguistic signs are of the second type, those which express a meaning.[5]

Husserl tells us that at the source of the concept of expression lies its communicative function.[6] He takes as the model of this function one person speaking to another. What occurs is that the speaker wishes to share with the listener a *meaning* and does so through the psychophysical act of speaking. But this sharing is possible only because the listener understands the intention of the speaker.[7] Verbal expression in its communicative function serves the listener as signs of the "thoughts" of the speaker, enabling the listener to share the psychic experiences of the speaker. This is the communicative or informative function of language par excellence. But for the listener to understand the information is not for him to directly grasp knowledge of the

4 Edmund Husserl, *Logical Investigations*, 2 vols., trans. J. N. Findlay (New York: Humanities Press, 1970), I, p. 250.
5 *Ibid.*, p. 269.
6 *Ibid.*, p. 276.
7 *Ibid.*, p. 277.

information; what the listener has is an apperception of the speaker as a person who expresses such-and-such. He "grasps" a signitive representation *as presented*, by the speaker, rather than having a direct intuition of the "thing" being spoken about.[8] We shall see the significance of this fact later.

An examination of this model shows us that further distinctions have to be made in an effort to describe it adequately. What is it that an expression expresses? The expression expresses a meaning, and the expression and the meaning which it expresses are distinct, since as a sign an expression is an expression of something other than itself. This something other is a meaning.[9] But also, as a sign it indicates or refers to something, an objectivity.

An act of expression is an act of meaning. An *act* of meaning, however, is not to be identified with meaning. Every such act of meaning involves meaning, but also a reference to an object. Meaning is only one aspect of an act of meaning. The expression refers to (names) the object by virtue of its meaning. At the same time the object never coincides with the meaning.[10]

We shall now further elaborate this aspect of the "referring to an object" of the expression or act of meaning. It has a two-sided structure: on the one hand we see that according to Husserl it is of the essence of every act of meaning that it has a reference to an object. Insofar as every expression means something, it is a meaning-intention. But as we know, meaning is an ideal and not a real type of being. So that although it is only because the expression means something that it can refer to an object, if the reference of the expression is only a meaning-intention, then it functions as an unrealized meaning-intention.[11] And this is always the case if there is no, or even if there is, an empty intuition of the object of reference (*Anschauunglearen*).[12] There is another side to the act of meaning which is in fact extra-essential to it, but has the fundamental logical relation to it of *fulfilling the intention*, thereby actualizing its objective reference.[13] This act is called the meaning-fulfilling act. Although the meaning-fulfilling act is not

[8] *Ibid.*, pp. 277–8.
[9] *Ibid.*, p. 281.
[10] *Ibid.*, p. 287.
[11] *Ibid.*, p. 280.
[12] *Ibid.*, p. 281.
[13] *Ibid.*

of the essence of the act of expression, it is perfectly clear that for Husserl the ideal is that every act of expression have as its terminus the meaning-fulfilling act.[14] The meaning-fulfilling acts are distinct from the acts of meaning, but they form a phenomenological unity.[15] This means that at the heart of expressive acts lies the actualization, the realization of the referential object by means of a direct intuition or fantasy image.

Let us summarize what is involved in the act of expressing a meaning insofar as we have elaborated it. There are four factors so far:

1. The meaning-intending act – the act intends a meaning.

2. The content of the act – a meaning. It is important to note the difference between points one and two; Husserl insists that the intending act and the meaning are not the same (the difference can be seen as that between the verb form and the noun form of the term "meaning.")

3. Reference to an objectivity meant. It is only because the act has a meaning that it can refer to an object, but the meaning as content and the object as meant are not the same.

4. Although not essential to the act of meaning (the meaning-intention), given with it is the possibility of the meaning-fulfillment. What fulfills the meaning-intention is the realization of the meaning by means of an intuitive perception or fantasy image of the object of reference. That is, bringing to presence of the object of reference is the meaning-fulfillment.

One more point needs to be clarified that is essential to our examination of Husserl's doctrine of language, but Husserl does not get around to examining this point until the "Fifth Investigation." It is, however, already implicit in the results of our investigation of the situation of the listener and the speaker. We said there that what in fact the listener obtains is an apperception of the speaker as a person who expresses such-and-such, and that what he grasps directly are word-sounds functioning as signs that represent, rather than having a direct intuition of, the "thing" being spoken about. Husserl goes on to articulate this by a further distinction that he makes in reference to how acts of consciousness are constituted. He says that there are in fact

14 *Ibid.*, pp. 280–281.
15 *Ibid.*, p. 282.

two *distinct* acts involved in the meaningful utterance of an expression; one act which forms the word and another which contributes meaning to the word.[16] Phenomenologically speaking every meaningful utterance involves the unity of those acts in which an expression taken physically is constituted, and those entirely different acts in which meaning is constituted.[17] To be sure, the acts are given as a unity, but it is important for us that they are not one and the same act. We shall see that it is the intentional nature of consciousness which unifies the acts. What we are concerned with here is that this distinction means that for Husserl language consists of meanings given across signs, that language carries meanings across signs. This has great bearing on our study since it points out a certain duality that Husserl must deal with.

We have already noted that, according to Husserl, the being of meaning is ideal, whereas the being of signs (word-sounds, marks, etc.) is empirical. This means that in language what has to occur to make it intelligible and communicable at all is that consciousness has to *interpret*, "transliterate" as it were, signs or marks in order that they be *meaningful*. Husserl feels that there is very little trouble in considering the necessary relations which meanings have to each other, since these are determined by certain logical structures which are of course of an ideal nature. And these structures, as holding among meanings, therefore determine the possible empirical relations of expressions. For this reason concludes Husserl, it is possible to have an *a priori* grammar.[18]

Since Husserl is doing phenomenology rather than metaphysics, he is not required to postulate a theory as to how specific meanings become associated with specific signs, something which has certainly been a knotty problem in the history of philosophy. What he is required to do, however, is to give a satisfactory account of how these diverse acts of consciousness (the constitution of meaning and the constitution of the sign) are unified. And from one perspective that task can be seen as showing how it is that meanings are *realized*. We already know that this is partially what is involved in point four mentioned above, the act of

16 *Ibid.*, pp. 582–6.
17 *Ibid.*, p. 583.
18 *Ibid.*, Section IV, pp. 493–532.

meaning-fulfillment. Our present task then is to see just how meaning-fulfilling acts function as the "bridge" of the ideal and the real, as well as the examination of the epistemological ground of fulfillment.

B. MEANING-FULFILLMENT

We have seen that it is the structure of every expression to be a meaning-intention that has an objective reference by means of its meaning. Also, even though not of the essence of an act of meaning as such, we have seen that determined logically there is associated with the meaning-intention the act of meaning-fulfillment. We must here pose two questions concerning meaning-fulfillment:

1. What is the function of this act?
2. How is this function carried out?

The function of the meaning-fulfilling act is just what its name implies; it is an act which fulfills the meaning-intending act, and thereby fulfills the meaning which is intended in the meaning-intention. It does so through its association with the referential object of the meaning-intention. This is a distinction of crucial importance. The function of the act of meaning-fulfillment is the actualization of the objective reference of the meaning-intending act.[19]

It is by means of the referential-object that the unity of the meaning-intention and the meaning-fulfilling act is accomplished. In the actualized reference (*Beziehung*) of the expression to its objectivity, the meaning-giving expression unites with the act of meaning-fulfillment.[20]

Husserl's description here is determined by the phenomenologically basic distinction between the meaning of an act of meaning and the referential object of an act of meaning, and it is a necessary distinction if the phenomena are to be accounted for. In its wake we can see a double consequence. First, it again emphasizes the ideality of meaning as such; an expression can be meaningful, make sense, present a meaning, without the object of

[19] *Ibid.*, p. 281.
[20] *Ibid.*

reference being actualized in a meaning-fulfilling act.[21] That is, understanding or comprehension in a broad sense is possible *without intuition* of what is understood. Secondly, it is by means of this distinction that logically every act of meaning-intention has associated with it an act of meaning-fulfillment, that it becomes explicable that all significative acts can be understood as being *founded acts*, and that those upon which they are founded are founding acts, understood as primordial acts of intuition. These founding acts are those which give, make present, in an original sense, the objects. This accounts for how objects of meaning-intending expressions, which as such are given originally by the only acts that can give objects originally, are acts of intuition.[22] In the later works of Husserl this intuitionist thesis that makes the epistemological teaching of the principle of all principles viable will be exploited to the fullest extent. That is, it is only because the relation between founded and founding acts of consciousness has been established in such a way that there is a point of coalescence between them (the objective reference of the signitive act) that the principle of all principles can be applied without making all "theoretical" acts of consciousness inconsistent with that principle. Cast into the language of traditional philosophy, Husserl's elaboration on meaning-intentions and meaning-fulfillment is supposed to come to grips with the question of the relationship of "concepts or thoughts" and corresponding "intuitions."[23] In the passage that we quoted from *Ideas* at the beginning of this chapter we can see that Husserl feels that he has resolved this problem in a satisfactory way and that he can therefore base the rest of his work on this foundation.

Carried out to its limits within an epistemological problematic, this becomes the question of truth and verification. It is to this topic that we shall now turn, first working our way through the linguistic strata that makes the question possible at all. We shall first look at the situation of language from a perspective other than the one we have used up to now by asking: what is it that an act of expression expresses insofar as it is a founded act?

Husserl says it is possible to bring all types of acts to expression,

---

[21] *Ibid.*, pp. 286, 303–4.
[22] *Ibid.*, pp. 290–1.
[23] *Ibid.*, p. 669.

and such expression gives us the meanings of the related language forms.[24] Every act has its own form of expression which is proper to it, and this is what is manifested in "propositional forms" of different types such as questions, wishes, judgments, etc. It is only because acts can be known in apperception as form and content that they can be brought to their corresponding forms of expression.[25] From this Husserl concludes the expression of language does not lie in mere words, but rather in expressing acts.[26] He sees the confirmation of this conception as lying in the pure symbolic function of the expressions; the fact that we can "understand the expression of an act of perception without ourselves perceiving anything, of a question without ourselves asking anything, etc."[27] That is, in communication we do not have only bare words presented, but also the thought-forms or their expressions.

This teaching means that understanding is possible *without* a corresponding intuition of any degree at all; the act of meaning-intention simply remains unfulfilled, but comprehension of the meaning is still possible. This is one extreme of the linguistic situation. At the other extreme, when the object of the intending act is really present, there occurs a coincidence (*Deckung*) of the expression and that which is expressed; the meaning associated with the words "fits" what is meant, and the thought-intention finds therein the fulfilling intuition. The language situation as here described sets the limits of gradations of the corresponding concept of verification: an expression which is understood solely by its form has a zero degree of possible verification corresponding to it, whereas one that is associated with a fulfilling intuition has the corresponding highest degree of verification. It is within the consideration of the concept of verification that it first becomes possible to talk about the concept of truth.

C. EVIDENCE AND TRUTH

It is irrelevant, says Husserl, whether the fulfilling intuition of a propositional act of meaning is a perception or merely a phantasy image, since it is in either case an objectivating presen-

---

[24] *Ibid.*, p. 675.
[25] *Ibid.*, p. 676.
[26] *Ibid.*
[27] *Ibid.*

tation of the object of reference and as such accomplishes the function of fulfillment.[28] But the achievement of fulfillment has gradations corresponding to the gradations of fullness of the intuitive acts themselves. All intuitive acts have fulfillment, but to a greater or lesser degree.[29] Even complete fulness of an act in the sphere of imagination lacks something in comparison with acts of perception; there exists a hierarchy of objectivating acts. Imagination, for example, is distinguished from perception in that it *does not give the thing itself,* not even a part of the thing. Imagination "gives only the image, which, so long as it remains the image, is never the thing (*Sache*) itself. The thing we owe to perception."[30]

Every perception has the quality of presenting the thing itself and not the image or re-presentation of the object. But not even all perceptions present their objects totally, completely. We have already seen that it is the nature of external perception to give its objects in profiles; in this sense perception also represents the object, but this representation is essentially different from that performed in the sphere of imagination since it represents through the self-presenting of the object, not as an image of the object.[31]

As we have previously noted, it is of the essence of purely significative intentions that they have no fullness.[32] To explain how the fulfillment of such significative intentions is nonetheless possible (that is, how an act of expression can be fulfilled) Husserl elaborates on the traditional conception of *adequatio rei ad intellectus.*

The presenting-intention (act), which has been brought to highest or final fullness by means of the complete, total perception, has posited therewith the genuine *adequatio rei ad intellectus.* The object is exactly as intended, is "really objective," or "given"; no more partial or unfulfilled intentions are implicated since the intention has been "exhausted" by its fulfillment.[33] And the

[28] *Ibid.*, p. 760.

[29] *Ibid.*, p. 761.

[30] *Ibid.*

[31] *Ibid.*, p. 762. Husserl in the *Beilage* elaborates on the distinction of inner and outer, evident and non-evident perceptions. It is perfectly clear that what he has in mind is nothing less than the distinctions of the realms of perception which will be elaborated in *Ideas.* It is not until then, however, that he brings forth the conceptual apparatus that enables him to make these distinctions successfully.

[32] *Ibid.*, p. 761.

[33] *Ibid.*, p. 762.

significative intention receives its fulfillment in an exactly correlative sense. The intellectus is the conceptual (*gedankliche*) intention, that of the meaning. The *adequatio* is realized when the intended objectivity is given, in the strong sense, to intuition exactly as it was thought and intended.[34]

Husserl follows out this theme of the *adequatio* in relation to the significative intention and the fulfilling perception in a reflection on the concept of verification. The concept of verification, says Husserl, refers exclusively to positing acts in relation to their posited fulfillment, *and finally to their fulfillment through perceptions*.[35] In this last mentioned instance is manifested the ideal of adequation – evidence.

Husserl makes the distinction between evidence in a loose and a rigorous sense.[36] It is possible to speak of grades of evidence, of lesser or greater degrees of evidence, whenever a positional intention receives its verification in a corresponding perception, and this perception is itself fulfilled to a lesser or greater extent. But Husserl restricts this everyday notion of evidence and uses the term only in its strongest and most precise sense: it refers to the act of complete fulfillment – synthesis in which the intention has absolute fullness given by the object itself. "Evidence itself, we said, is the act of this most perfect synthesis of fulfillment."[37] The objective correlate of evidence is called "Being in the sense of truth, or simply truth."[38]

To really understand the full force that this notion of evidence and its relation to truth has for Husserl we must recall that what is at stake for Husserl is nothing less than what motivates the entire project of the *Logische Untersuchungen*: the necessary understanding of the ideality and objectivity of truth. It is this contention, that truth is ideal and thereby objective, that necessitates for Husserl the refutation of psychologism which is the first aim of the work. In Husserl's understanding, if truth and its origin is merely empirical, it is impossible. And if it is impossible, so is pure logic as well as all other sciences of the ideal, and ultimately, even all empirical sciences, since they too are de-

[34] *Ibid.*
[35] *Ibid.*, p. 765.
[36] *Ibid.*
[37] *Ibid.*
[38] *Ibid.*

pendent upon the ideality and objectivity of truth. But Husserl sees that he must avoid the other extreme also, that of logicism. He cannot make truth and logic into idealities in the Platonic sense, for he feels that this would lead to the absurd claim that practical logic and empirical science have no efficacy whatsoever. Each of these alternatives he says is contradicted by the "things themselves." There must therefore be possible a mode of *experience* of truth whereby truth can still manifest its ideality. It is the concept of evidence which is to fulfill this function for Husserl, that of giving the experience of truth while at the same time allowing it to retain its ideality. Husserl says in the *Prolegomena*:

> ... evidence is rather nothing but the "experience" of truth. Truth is of course only experienced in the sense in which something ideal can be an experience in a real act.[39]

Evidence is an experience (*Erlebnis*), an act of consciousness. What sort of an act? "... evidence is called a seeing, a grasping of the self-given (true) state of affairs, or, as we say with tempting equivocation, the Truth." [40] As an act of consciousness, a seeing, an insight, evidence must have an object; this is demanded by the intentional nature of consciousness. The object of evidence is truth itself.

> The experience of the agreement between meaning and what is itself present, meant, between the actual sense of an assertion and the self-given state of affairs, is inward evidence: the Idea of this agreement is truth, whose ideality is also its objectivity.[41]

D. EVIDENCE AND THE METAPHYSICS OF PRESENCE

It is impossible to minimize the importance of this concept of evidence in the thought of Husserl. We agree with Lauer that it is the fundamental problem of Husserl's whole philosophic endeavor, and that Husserl himself recognized this as early as the *Logische Untersuchungen*.[42] How are we to understand this concept and the key role it plays for Husserl's thought in terms of our own epistemological investigation? We maintain that the

---

[39] *Ibid.*, p. 194.
[40] *Ibid.*, p. 195.
[41] *Ibid.*
[42] Quenton Lauer, *Phenomenology: Its Genesis and Prospect* (New York: Harper & Row, 1965), p. 47.

reason the concept of evidence holds the central place that it does is because evidence is the epistemological moment of presence, the moment of absolute presence in which Being is given as such, known as what it is, and also *known* that it is known as such. It is therefore the highest epistemological moment, and in the Husserlean thought this means that it is also the metaphysical moment, the moment of the presence of being. It is in evidence, presupposing a significative act, that there is the unification of thought and being, the metaphysical moment itself.

By showing that it is presence that is the key notion that makes evidence what it is, let us now see explicitly how the concept of evidence manifests Husserl's unity with and dependence upon the metaphysics of presence. In showing this we shall be demonstrating that at the very heart of the Husserlean teaching lies the fundamental agreement with the line of philosophical thought which we have characterized as the metaphysics of presence. We shall think through an interpretation which gives four modes in which presence is integral to the notion of evidence.

1. Evidence is possible only when the object is immanent to the stream of the intending consciousness. Immanence here means nothing other than presence; the intended object is totally present to the intending consciousness. It is so by way of being at one with the intention. The intention has "fullness" because the object, given to it completely, also completely fulfills the intention. The intending refers to nothing "other," nothing alien, nothing absent to what is given; the object in total presence. This is *total presence*; the object is totally present to the intention, but also the intention is totally present "in" the object, is exhausted by it. There is nothing of the intention which is absent; the intention is fulfilled in the object as well as by the object. This is the presence of the fulfilling act of consciousness to itself, as intention and object.

But, of course, *this* presence is not yet evidence; it is a necessary condition of evidence. The reason it is not itself evidence is that the notion of evidence is related to significative acts, that is, acts of language, since it is these acts for which evidence *is* evidence.

2. Evidence is presence of an act of fulfillment (which itself has fullness) to an act of signification which is by its essence an "empty intention." It is the coinciding synthesis of these acts

which is evidence. As previously noted, the referential object which is necessary to every act of meaning provides the possibility of the unification of acts of different types. What makes the act of evidence as the coinciding synthesis possible is that the object being spoken about can also be seen, pointed out. It is presupposed of course that in order for it to provide evidence, the "seeing" has been total, complete, an act which has fulfillment. In other words, that the perceiving act has been brought to fulfillment. This means that evidence is an act of making present of the fulfilling act to the significative act, of bringing to presence one act to the other as a coinciding synthesis. Evidence makes itself present by bringing the two different types of acts, that of signifying and that of perceiving, into the presence of each other, and the making present of this presence is the act of evidence. We shall return to this function of evidence as making present in this second sense, since Husserl's fundamental notion of language (which culminates in evidence) revolves around this conception.

3. Truth as ideal is realized as the correlate of evidence, and evidence, from this viewpoint, is nothing other than the bringing into presence of truth. Truth is brought to presence in the act of evidence; consciousness is in "direct contact" with truth. But for Husserl, truth is the manifestation of being itself, and being as present "in" consciousness is absolute being and absolute presence.

The relation of being and truth, as Husserl makes clear, is that of two sides of the same meaning. Being is manifested as truth; that which is manifested in truth is absolute being. The *experience* of truth, the experience which brings absolute being to presence, is the experience of evidence. Evidence as the experience which manifests truth is the act which brings truth and absolute being into presence. Evidence brings to presence what is, as it is, without otherness, and thereby negates absence and negativity. Evidence is the experience of absolute being absolutely present across truth.

4. Finally, it is important to note that Husserl stresses that evidence is an *act*. He describes it as a coinciding synthesis (*Deckungssynthesis*). As an act of consciousness it has an intentional structure. It is from this point of view of evidence as an intentional act that we propose that it becomes explicably why

Husserl sees evidence as the highest epistemological moment, the moment of the *adequatio,* the moment of truth.

It is because evidence as an intentional act is the only act of consciousness that coincides with itself totally; it is the only act of consciousness in which the intention and the object which realizes the meaning are one, and given at once, *as one.* The referential object in the structure of the evidential act of meaning is the point of the *Deckungssynthesis;* but precisely the realization of this object is nothing other than evidence itself. The third structural component of the act is the meaning, and the meaning of the act of evidence is truth. And as we have seen, evidence is nothing other than the experience of truth itself. We see therefore that thought all the way through, the act of evidence has as its meaning the experience of truth which is itself evidence, and which is realized in the object as *evidence.*

It is in this triple coincidence that is to be understood what is remarkable about the notion of evidence; it is the act of meaning which coincides with itself; in it the structure of the act of meaning "collapses," closes in upon itself. No act of evidence requires evidence for itself as an experience, since it is essentially at one with itself. This is perhaps the sense in which the term "self-evident" is to be taken in its strongest sense. The act, the meaning, and the object are given as the same, and given through and to itself as such. Every act of evidence is absolutely present to itself. Epistemologically this means that the act of evidence, the act which is at one with itself, is the act which manifests presence as the absolute criterion of knowledge, while at the same time being that object of knowledge itself.

It is in these four ways that we have thought through the meaning of the *adequatio rei ad intellectus* as the notion of presence. This is the remarkable epistemology which is at the heart of the Husserlean teaching, an epistemology which grounds itself in the concept of evidence. It in turn rests on, and has its meaning through, the metaphysics of presence.

E. LANGUAGE AND CONSCIOUSNESS

We have seen that the whole notion of evidence is tied to the understanding of language for Husserl, and we have suggested that it is this relationship which manifests for the first time Husserl's reliance on the metaphysics of presence. Husserl returns again and again to the question of evidence in his later works, and he does elaborate and certaintly goes beyond that doctrine of evidence that he presents in the *Logische Untersuchungen*. But I propose that what brings about at least part of the continual problematic is that Husserl never really goes back to think through the question of language again, and it is this that is the underlying source of the whole doctrine of evidence. Merleau-Ponty remarks that as systematic a thinker as Husserl was, he never seems to have really developed a theory of language in any intricate or completed way: the question is never really revived for him after the *Logische Untersuchungen*.[43] There are two components of this teaching on language which suggest themselves as somehow at the root of the necessity for the constant rethinking of phenomenology by Husserl, but which themselves were not called into question by Husserl, and in that way were essentially presupposed in every other "phenomenological problem."

1. The relationship of the word, as sign, to the meaning of the sign. We have seen that for Husserl the constitution of the word and the constitution of the meaning are two different acts. This means that the relation of the sign to its meaning is "unessential," that the sign has no influence, *does not contribute to the meaning of the word*. Husserl's understanding is that it is the meaning as ideal that determines the possible combination of signs into meaningful utterances – this is what is at the heart of his contention that it is possible to create an *a priori* grammar which must hold true for every language. Since it is the meaning which is essential, whereas the words themselves are contingent, if one can deduce or adduce the necessary relationships among meanings, then one will have determined necessarily the relations possible among certain types of signs which express their meanings.

[43] Maurice Merleau-Ponty, *Signs*, trans. R. McCleary (Evanston: Northwestern University Press, 1964), p. 84.

It is evident that Husserl's understanding of the relationship of meaning and sign is not at all compatible with the understanding brought forth by the modern science of linguistics, particularly the structural linguistics initiated by de Saussure.[44] For the structuralists, language first of all forms a system, and a system of words no less than a system of meanings. And it is impossible to isolate one element of the expressive act from the other elements. Structuralism teaches that each word has a meaning which is determined by its place in the system of words and meanings, in relation to all of the others, both directly and dialectically.[45] "Every determination is a negation," said Spinoza. A determination in principle can take place only within a system; what is determined is done so in regard to the other elements of the system. For example, what could the term "maroon" mean without being set in a system of the concepts of colors? Precisely, its meaning has to be determined as somewhere between red and purple, etc.

This is not the place to elaborate on the discoveries of structural linguistics, nor even to show that Husserl's doctrine of expression and meaning fails to account for the phenomena, although we have indicated this. Derrida, through his investigation of signification accomplishes this critique in a detailed manner. It is interesting to point out that both Heidegger and Merleau-Ponty, who have Husserl at the source of their thought, have a doctrine of language much closer to the structuralist notion of language than to that of Husserl.[46] In the structuralist notion of language what is at stake is the relationship of presence and absence.[47] The meaning of the term, and the term itself are *present*, but only in relation to the whole system which manifests itself as an absence. The meaning of the term is given against the absence which is the ground of the presence of the meaning and determines it. Through the meaning which is made present, the absent, as the system of language, manifests itself in order that meaning be presented. The meaning of the word is present in the word, but never absolutely,

[44] JoAnn Fuchs, "The Philosophy of Language of Maurice Merleau-Ponty," unpublished Master's Thesis (University Park, Pa.: The Pennsylvania State University, 1968), p. 23.

[45] *Ibid.*, pp. 23–24.

[46] Merleau-Ponty, *Signs*, p. 39, *et passim.*

[47] *Ibid.*, p. 39.

since the presence of the word and the meaning is always condi-
tioned by the absence of the system of which they are a part and
which is the condition of their manifestation. By viewing language
as a system of interdetermined words and meanings and structures, what is revealed is the co-primordiality of presence and
absence; that is to say, the *non-absolute* nature of the *presence
of meaning*. Meaning as presence can mean only in relation to
absence. An investigation of language itself therefore undermines
the doctrine of the metaphysics of presence, that doctrine which
Husserl first articulates with his investigation of language.

2. There is a second unresolved problematic which opens up
for Husserl from the work on language in the *Logische Untersuchungen*. In maintaining that there are two different acts of
constitution involved in the linguistic act, Husserl must also
maintain what is at best an ambiguous teaching concerning the
nature of consciousness. This teaching really allows that there are
two different types of acts of consciousness, or what is the same
thing, that consciousness works in two different ways. On the
one hand, the word-sound is constituted in consciousness by means
of the activization of the hyletic data of consciousness. This is
perfectly straightforward, and we shall call this the interpretive
act of consciousness since the meaning (the object meant) becomes
manifest through the interpretation of the data of consciousness
to "mean." But on the other hand, Husserl also points out that
the meaning of a linguistic act is constituted in a completely
different act from the constitution of the word-sound. Here
meaning is constituted in the act of meaning which refers to the
object intended. This second act of consciousness functions so as
to represent the object, making the object present through the
intention as what is meant. This second type of act of consciousness we shall call representational; meaning is constituted by
means of representational consciousness of the intended object.
There is no mention here of hyletic data, of the interpretation of
data into meaning, but rather of the direct representation of
meaning in the intended object. It is in the teaching on evidence
that both of these types of consciousness are integrated, but it is
an unsure integration, one which perhaps is at the bottom of
Husserl's constant discontent with his doctrine of evidence. In
the *Logische Untersuchungen* Husserl makes the doctrine of evi-

dence hang directly on the notion of absolute presence and does so by making of it the synthetic act which covers two previous acts of consciousness. One way of interpreting that is to say that the act of evidence synthesizes two different *types* of acts of consciousness, both consciousness as interpretation and consciousness as representation. But Husserl must give a priority to consciousness as representation since this has a direct relation to the whole notion of the primordiality of presence. The act of evidence itself, therefore, is a representative act, a *re-presenting* act, an act of making present as was shown above. But how is this possible when one of the factors synthesized is in principle something which does not lend itself to presence, where meaning is achieved as a result of interpretation across signs, where meaning is not directly present, where it is necessarily absent?

This is a very complex problem and I do not pretend to have exhausted it here. But I do suggest that it is this dual nature of consciousness, which Husserl must adhere to in order to account for the phenomenon of language as he understands it, that is at the root of this problem. It is interesting to note that Husserl himself comes to see the problem in terms of presence explicitly when he reflects upon his teaching of evidence in the *Formal and Transcendental Logic* as well as the *Cartesian Meditations*. Adequation in the sense used in the *Logische Untersuchungen* is dropped as a characteristic of evidence and instead evidence becomes the *ideal limit* of every intentional act of consciousness.[48] This can be interpreted to mean that what Husserl is trying to do is to unify consciousness and have all consciousness be of the same type, in principle interpretational. Presence is till here a guiding thought, but rather than have evidence be the highest epistemological moment, it now becomes the ideal moment which is contained as an ideal in *every* act of consciousness.

Already in seeing evidence as being explicable only in terms of the world as being a *system* of evidence, Husserl is coming much nearer to the type of understanding that maintains that language is a system. For what is indicated here, although certainly not completely thought out, is that even evidence as structurally dependent upon the whole system of evidence and the world as

[48] Husserl, *Cartesian Meditations*, Section 28.

evidence giving, manifests the co-primordiality of absence and presence. That is, that even the teaching on evidence which is built upon the notion of the metaphysics of presence turns upon itself to deny this very same metaphysical teaching.

CHAPTER IV

TEMPORALITY AND PRESENCE

A. THE PROBLEMATIC OF TIME

At the heart of Husserl's phenomenological teaching lies his doctrine of time. It is in many ways his most historically important research. There are three interrelated reasons for making such a statement.

1. Husserl's research on the problematic of time leads to the first truly unique systematic doctrine of time since the topic was brought to the philosophic foreground by Aristotle.

2. The reason that this uniqueness is possible is because this teaching is thoroughly and completely phenomenological. That is, it becomes possible only by means of the methodological and epistemological approaches so carefully prepared by Husserl to make accessible the reign of pure consciousness to phenomenological research. Husserl shows that not even for his most immediate predecessor, Brentano, is it possible to avoid those problems and enigmas put forth by time, since the development of phenomenology had not yet been accomplished and had not elaborated the insights that would make this possible.

3. It has been the Husserlean teaching on time which more than anything else has been carried forward by the existentialist thinkers, particularly Heidegger, Sartre, and Merleau-Ponty. From Husserl's insights on time has come the impetus for the contemporary existentialist ontologies. Of course they carried this teaching of time far beyond what Husserl himself saw as legitimate; in fact to some extent against the wishes of Husserl himself. But as we shall indicate, it is precisely from these insights drawn by Husserl himself that the "explosion" of the doctrine of time has lead into existentialist ontology.

This chapter will take into consideration these three points, but its main goal will be to demonstrate that in one of his greatest phenomenological researches, that on time, Husserl in fact contradicts his intended movement of this thought as being in accord with the metaphysics of presence. It is in the investigation and description of time that Husserl reveals the co-primordiality of presence and absence within the ultimate strata of the constitutive process. This is revealed despite the fact that Husserl does not think to embrace this conclusion, since it is contrary to that underlying metaphysical notion which he carries through on the epistemological plane. In the teaching on time as in the teaching on language we shall see how Husserl's phenomenological investigations are at odds with the overriding considerations which he brings to bear.

There is a source to the problematic of time in the history of philosophy; Aristotle raises it to the level of an object of serious contemplation in the *Physics*. Aristotle realized the legitimacy of the question, "If there were no soul, could there still be time?" It is in his answer to this question that we see the line of thought that will dominate Western thinking for the next two thousand years. For Aristotle time is a real process, independant of subjectivity and given as a real attribute of motion. Time is the enumeration possible because of the successive nature (before-after) of movement, with the "now" being the pivotal point that is the end of the past, the beginning of the future, as well as the link between the two. Not only does time measure movement, but since movement and time define each other, movement can also measure time. This is the heart of the predominant teaching on time that is in effect until the work of Kant.

It almost seems that to go from Aristotle's teaching on time to that of Kant is simply to state the reverse. And indeed, what is at stake for Kant is in some sense the reverse of Aristotelian metaphysics on epistemological grounds. It is hardly surprising then that for Kant, although time is no less empirically real than for Aristotle, it does not have its existence as an attribute of movement nor of any other "objective" entity. It is the real form of inner intuition, and therefore, as Kant argues from the elucidation of space, the real form of any attributes whatsoever. But of course Kant denies time a claim to absolute reality; he argues for the empirical reality and the transcendental ideality of time.[1]

Despite these seemingly irreconcilable differences about the nature of time there is a remarkable similarity in the work of Aristotle and Kant concerning the derivative effects of the nature of time. For both Aristotle and Kant there is only one time; it has its revealed source in the relation "before-after," and since for Kant there can be no intuition of pure time, the intuitions of time for both are dependent upon the intuition of movement. It seems that despite the "Copernican Revolution," that Kant, through his disclaiming of the old metaphysical enterprise, remains within it, and this shows in the teaching on time. Heidegger supports this interpretation when he says:

> When we analyse the Aristotelian conception, it will likewise become clear, as we go back, that the Kantian account of time operates within the structure which Aristotle has set forth; this means that Kant's basic ontological orientation remains that of the Greeks, in spite of all the distinctions which arise in the new inquiry.[2]

It is from this conception of time that the work of Husserl makes its break to bring forth his radically new teaching, one we shall see, which calls forth a new ontological understanding, not only of time, but of the privileged status of being as presence.

B. TIME AS A PHENOMENOLOGICAL DATUM

In *Ideas* Husserl gives only a very marginal and brief account of time and the bearing it has to phenomenology (see, particularly, Sec. 81, 118). It is also given very brief treatment in the *Cartesian Meditations* (Sec. 18). But the brevity of the treatment should not be taken as a sign that the topic is unimportant at this stage of his thinking. To the contrary, Husserl makes it quite clear that time is literally at the heart of phenomenology:

> Time is the name for a completely self-contained sphere of problems and one of exceptional difficulty. ... The transcendental "Absolute" which we have laid bare through the reductions is in truth not ultimate; it is something which in a certain profound and wholly unique sense constitutes itself, and has its primeval source in what is ultimately and truly absolute.[3]

---

[1] Kant, *Critique*, p. B52.
[2] Martin Heidegger, *Being and Time*, trans. Macquarrie and Robinson (New York: Harper & Row, 1962), p. 49.
[3] Husserl, *Ideas*, p. 236.

This ultimate to which Husserl refers is nothing other than time, and Husserl considers his research on time essentially accomplished by the lectures which he completed in 1905.[4] This means that it is completely legitimate for us to think through this work as the Husserlean teaching on time. Although Husserl had not yet at this point worked out the methodological approach to phenomenology which he sets out in *Ideas*, in retrospect it is clear that it is through intentional analysis and strict phenomenological description that Husserl presents the essential characteristics of time.

As do Aristotle and Kant, Husserl starts with objective time, the manifestation of time in nature, what we shall call cosmic time. But he takes cosmic time as a phenomenon. Unlike Aristotle and Kant however, Husserl notes the manifestation of another time, the time of *Erlebnis*, lived time, time and duration appearing as such. Cosmic time is given in, by, and with, transcendent objectivity, and is therefore excluded, bracketed by the phenomenological epoché, even though it can be considered as "appearing as such."[5] This does not mean that it is denied, or declared a mere myth; it means that we must restrict ourselves to the consideration of time as a phenomenological datum. What remains as the residue of the phenomenological reduction is an absolute datum, the immanent time of the flow of consciousness.

The phenomenological data are the apprehensions of time, the lived experiences in which the temporal in the Objective sense appears. Again, phenomenologically given are the moments of lived experience which specifically establish apprehensions of time as such, and therefore, establish if the occasion should arise, the specific temporal content (that which conventional nativism calls the primordially temporal).[6]

The task which Husserl sets for himself is to clarify the *a priori* of time, and to do this through an investigation of time-consciousness. On this level, for Husserl it is the same task to seek to clarify the essence of time and to seek the origin of time. This origin, in our sphere of investigation, cannot be psychological since we are investigating the *a priori* as such.[7] The question of

---

[4] *Ibid.*

[5] Edmund Husserl, *The Phenomenology of Internal Time Consciousness*, ed. Heidegger, trans. J. Churchill (Bloomington: Indiana University Press, 1964), p. 23.

[6] *Ibid.*, p. 24.

[7] *Ibid.*, p. 28.

the essence and the origin of time can only be resolved through
the determination of the constitution of the lived time of experience. It may indeed then turn out that there is given a relation
which shows how phenomenological time is connected with objective time; but this is an association which must arise out of the
phenomenological data itself.

Let us consider an example within the phenomenological
sphere. What does listening to a melody mean? A melody is made
up of tones, and clearly not all of the tones of a melody can be
given or heard simultaneously. If such were even conceivable it
would be at best a noise that I hear and not a melody. But even a
tone is not given all at once; it is given as a flow, it has a beginning
and has an end. Only one "part" of it can be heard *now*.[8] But the
tone I hear (as well as the melody) is given as a unified object that,
since it is not given all at once, but rather as a succession, must
have duration. That is, it endures across time. Since it appears
as a unity to consciousness, this consciousness itself must be a
unity which can encompass the object as it appears.[9] It is here,
in the presence of unity that a deeper analysis of the constitutive
elements in this experience must begin. Husserl delimits the
object of the analysis by saying:

> Since Objective temporality is always phenomenologically constituted
> and is present for us as Objectivity and moment of an Objectivity ac-
> cording to the mode of appearance only through this constitution, a
> phenomenological analysis of time cannot explain the constitution of time
> without reference to the constitution of the temporal Object. By temporal
> Objects, in this *particular sense*, we mean Objects which are not only
> unities in time but also include temporal extension in themselves.[10]

I am conscious of this tone, this immanent temporal object. It is
given, and I am conscious of it as "long as" any phase of it
appears as being given *now*.[11] The tone appears in a continuous
flux, but as different modes within this flux since I am conscious
of the beginning point of the tone and the interval from then to
"now." And when the tone has ended, in being conscious of its
"end-point" as now, I am still conscious of the tone in retention,
as "having been," and of having been of a unitary duration. The

---

8 *Ibid.*, pp. 43–44.
9 *Ibid.*, p. 42.
10 *Ibid.*, p. 43.
11 *Ibid.*, p. 44.

sound remains the same, but its "modes of appearance" change.
It is important to note that the experience is not that of discreet
moments of sound which are then arbitrarily associated in continuity. Says Husserl:

> The object retains its place; even so does the sound retain its time. Its
> temporal point is unmoved, but the sound vanishes into the remoteness of
> consciousness; the distance from the generative now becomes even greater.
> The sound itself is the same, but "in the way that" it appears, the sound
> is continually different.[12]

The object and its duration are not one and the same, precisely
since the object is the same, has identity, for the entire period of
its duration.[13] But this consciousness of the identity of the object
is possible only because there is consciousness of the duration.
Like all consciousness, it is an intentional consciousness. And this
intentionality is the key to an understanding of how it is possible
to perceive both the now-point of the tone and the phases of the
duration of the tone which are already past in a gradated series.[14]
This gradated series, or running-off phenomenon, is given in a
temporal perspective of the duration, and it is the perspective
which is always given from the now-point.

The modes of running-off of an immanent temporal object have
a beginning, a source-point, as Husserl calls it, and it is this which
is characterized as *now*. Of course there is ever a new phase
of the object which is characterized as now, and each new phase
serves as a source point.[15] This means that there is a constantly
expanding continuity of pasts, each of which is intentionally
related as a retention to the now, with at some indeterminate
point, the "earliest" retention dropping off and thereby, although
certainly "in the past," no longer having the character of a
retention. It is only because of this phenomenon of retention that
it is possible to hear a melody (or even a tone) at all.[16] This is
perfectly obvious since it is of the very essence of a melody to be
dependent as a whole on its constituent parts unfolding in time,
rather than being a series of discreet sensations. The parts of the

[12] *Ibid.*, p. 45.
[13] *Ibid.*
[14] *Ibid.*, p. 47.
[15] *Ibid.*, p. 50.
[16] *Ibid.*, p. 51.

melody are not simultaneous while at the same time constituting a unity.

In fact our analysis is far from complete in consideration of the temporal duration of the immanent object. If the perception properly so called is only of the now, the fact remains that the now functions as not only a limit of retentions, but in exactly the same way as a limit of protentions, for it functions not only in relation to apprehension of the past, but also of the future insofar as it is the now which has a futural implication.[17] In this sense, retentions and protentions function and are apprehended as the ideal limit of the now, and these are not added on as after-thoughts in the act of consciousness; the temporally constitutive acts which constitute the present also constitute the past and future as a unified structure.

> This implies that an act which claims to give a temporal object itself must contain in itself "now-apprehensions," "past-apprehensions," and the like and, in fact, in a primordially constitutive way.[18]

C. THE NOW

The mode of consciousness in which the now is given is neither retentional nor protentional despite the fact that the now cannot be given without these modes. Rather, the now is given in a primal impression. This impression is the source which begins the temporal constitutive spread of the enduring object, the spread consisting of the adhesion of protentions and retentions, the "running-off" phenomenon.[19] This *now* gives the object in *bodily self-presence*.[20] Therefore the *now* has an epistemological priority as the source of every consciousness of a temporally enduring object. This primal impression, the now, is the very source of *objectification*.

The now is of course the present. So it is in the present that the object is given in bodily self-presence. This notion is absolutely central for Husserl. It is at the heart of his epistemology for several reasons. Since it is in the present that the object is given in bodily self-presence, all modifications of the originary con-

---

17 *Ibid.*, p. 62.
18 *Ibid.*
19 *Ibid.*, p. 51.
20 *Ibid.*, p. 50.

sciousness can be traced back to this originating event through reflection and recollection, making the object in its mode of givenness accessible because of its temporal grounding.

The now is the moment of bodily self-presence. It is here that we must most strongly make the connection between "present" and "presence." It is only in the now-as-the-present that the object can be manifested in its presence *in the original*, as what it is, embodied or filled-out. The bodily self-presence of the object is its original presence, its primordial presence and manifestation of its being. After this, everything becomes *re*-presented, an image, bodiless, rather than "the real thing." Sartre gives us an insight as to how we must understand the relation of "present" and "presence" by referring us to the soldier or pupil who replies "present" at roll call. Present is opposed to *absent* as well as to past or future.[21]

We have seen in the investigation that we carried out in the first chapter that it is direct intuition that gives the object, and that primordial dator intuitions are those which give the object in its bodily self-presence. It is the notion of primal impression that Husserl works through in order to think out the meaning of "now." It is as absolute presence, that is, the presence of the object of intuition in consciousness in the present that this notion of primal impression has meaning for Husserl.[22]

Conversely ... we are led back to certain original experiences, to "impressions" which exhibit experiences that in the phenomenological sense are *absolutely primordial*. ... They are primordial in the sense in which concrete experiences can be that at all. For closer inspection reveals in their concreteness only *one*, but that always a continuously flowing *absolute primordial phase*, that of the living *now*.[23]

The content of every primal impression is that which is designated as the now, and its function in constituting objectivity is brought to light in an investigation of reproductive memory (which is not the same as retention; it is the memory in the reflective sense of which we usually speak when we say, I remember something).[24] The memory of a perception, for example, implies the reproduction of an earlier perception of an object as having

[21] Sartre, *Being and Nothingness*, p. 121.
[22] Husserl, *Time Consciousness*, Sections 16 and 17.
[23] Husserl, *Ideas*, p. 221.
[24] Husserl, *Time Consciousness*, p. 57.

been present; it is now given in relation to the actual now in the act of remembering. This memory then involves the presentification of a previously enduring object now.[25] This object of memory retains a unity as an objectivity somehow related to this now. How is this possible? In fact, this is to raise the question of how is there an Objective time at all. As Husserl formulates the problematic:

> Time is motionless and yet it flows. In the flow of time, in the continuous sinking away in the past, there is constituted a non-flowing, absolutely fixed identical Objective time. This is the problem.[26]

We have seen previously how Husserl accounts for the identity of the immanent object through the intentionality of the temporalizing consciousness. What is at stake now is how the temporal flow itself allows identity.[27] Husserl works out this problematic very carefully and systematically. He realizes perfectly well that the whole notion of objectivity rests upon his result.

There are two moments upon which the objectivation of temporal objects rests. True or "real" identity is not accomplished by identity in regard to content; even if the content of sensations belonging to the different actual now-point of the object remain qualitatively unaltered, there is still a difference. This difference is a "phenomenological difference which corresponds to the absolute temporal position."[28] According to Husserl this difference is the primal source of the individuality of the "this." And that means the primal source of the absolute temporal position. Each and every phase of the modification has essentially the same qualitative content and temporal moment, although they are modified. Also each phase has the same temporal moment so that by means of it, "the subsequent apprehension of identity is made possible: this on the side of sensation, or of the foundation of apprehension."[29] The true objectivation, the apprehension in its different parts is sustained by these different moments.

> One aspect of the Objectivation finds its support purely in the qualitative content of the material of sensation. This yields the temporal matter, e.g., the sound. This matter is held identically in the flux of the modifi-

25 *Ibid.*, pp. 58–59.
26 *Ibid.*, p. 89.
27 *Ibid.*, p. 88.
28 *Ibid.*, p. 90.
29 *Ibid.*, p. 91.

cations of the past. A second aspect of the Objectivation arises from the apprehension of the representatives of the temporal positions (Zeit-stellenrepraesentanton). This apprehension is also continuously retained in the flux of the modification.[30]

Such then is how temporal objectivities are constituted as described through the analysis of phenomenological time. Every individual object given as an enduring temporal object immanent to consciousness, whether transcendent or not, is constituted as a unity as a result of the constituted unity of the flow of time itself. We have then the constitution of temporal objects as well as the constitution of time. There remains only to consider the constituting or constitutive flux itself which is not itself constituted. It is this flux which Husserl names absolute subjectivity. It alone is never objectified, but attains its unity through its objectivating function. It is the source of that primal sensation, the moment of bodily presence which is the heart of temporality and of objectivity and the phenomenological epistemology which depends upon it.

We can only say that this flux is something which we name in conformity with what is constituted, but it is nothing temporally "objective." It is absolute subjectivity and has the absolute property of something to be denoted metaphorically as "flux," as a point of actuality, primal source-point, that from which springs the "now," and so on.[31]

D. THE TEMPORAL HORIZONS

Subjectivity is temporality, and temporality is the source of Objectivity. This is the essential metaphysical doctrine which Husserl teaches in contrast to all previous teachings on the nature of time. In Aristotle's metaphysical scheme time is not given a fundamental place because of its transient nature; it is derivative and does not lead to being. Time has no function as a source of synthesis of either knowing or being. Kant also deprives time of a metaphysical priority for essentially the same reason; it can never belong to being in itself, it has no place within the sphere of the absolute.

Time is essential to the phenomenological teaching because only in the now-point of the temporal flow does phenomenology

[30] *Ibid.*
[31] *Ibid.*, p. 100.

find the source of its basic epistemological criterion for the validity of any objectivity whatsoever, the evidential vision, the immediate presence of being. But is this really the case? Husserl makes it perfectly clear that the now-point is the moment of living presence, primal sensation, and the condition of what he will call in *Ideas* primordial dator consciousness. But Husserl has also made it perfectly clear that the now is not possible without the concurrent appearance of retention and protention, the horizons of the temporal dimensions. As Husserl points out in his criticism of Bretano's theory of time, it is a patent absurdity to claim that the past is present.[32]

According to the epistemological teaching of Husserl, the epistemological moment is the moment of living presence given in intuition and this is the only possible mode of originary consciousness. In arguing for the precedence of "impression" over "retention," Husserl shows very clearly why this point is important in his entire doctrine on time. It is necessary to make retention somehow secondary or derivative, since if it were co-primordial the whole doctrine of the privileged status of being as presence would be called into question. He states clearly and precisely that it is impossible for retention to be an originary consciousness.

> What is remembered *is*, of course, not now; otherwise it would not be something that has been but would be actually present. And in memory (retention) what is remembered is not given as now: otherwise memory or retention would not be just memory but perception (or primal impression) .... "Past" and "now" exclude each other.[33]

However, in his teaching on time where he discusses retention and protention, Husserl affirms that retention is an originary consciousness: "The intuition of the past itself cannot be a symbolization; it is an originary consciousness."[34] It seems then that Husserl holds a thesis that maintains one position and ascribes to the phenomenon a characteristic that demands another position. Let us investigate this seeming contradiction more deeply.

In his phenomenological description, where he differentiates reproductive (secondary) memory from retention, a quite different understanding of the actual being of retention is presented from

[32] *Ibid.*, p. 33.
[33] *Ibid.*, pp. 56–57.
[34] *Ibid.*, p. 53.

what he had previously maintained, and necessarily so in order to make the phenomenon of memory explicable. In speaking of the *adequate* perception of temporal objects Husserl says:

> An Objectivity such as a melody cannot itself be originarily given except as "perceived" in this form. The constituted act constructed from now-consciousness and retentional consciousness, is *adequate perception of the temporal Object*.[35]

From this Husserl draws a conclusion which forces him to reduce the definitive difference he had decreed between the "now" and the "past."

> In an ideal sense, then, perception (impression) would be the phase of consciousness which constitutes the pure now, and memory every other phase of the continuity. But this is just an ideal limit .... Moreover, it is also true that even this ideal now is not something *toto caelo* different from the not-now ....[36]

Again, in contrasting perception and reproduction in the sense of reproductive memory Husserl is forced to draw conclusions which are diametrically opposed to those he put forth concerning the derivative nature of retentional consciousness.

> However, if we call perception the act in which all "origination" lies, which constitutes originarily, then primary remembrance is perception ... it is the essence of primary remembrance to bring this new and unique moment to primary, direct intuition, just as it is the essence of the perception, of the now to bring the now directly to intuition.[37]

The descriptive analysis becomes even more self-evidently deviant from the thesis which Husserl originarily proposed when he turns from the consciousness of enduring objects to the givenness of duration and succession themselves. Concerning the consciousness of succession we find that " ... it is an originary dator (*gebenis*) consciousness; it is the 'perception' of this succession."[38] From the nature of the givenness involved in succession insofar as this givenness necessarily involves retention, Husserl concludes that, "Retention constitutes the living horizon of the now ...."[39] Finally, Husserl says of the process of succession: "The entire succession is given originally as presence (*Praesenz*)."[40]

[35] *Ibid.*, p. 60.
[36] *Ibid.*, p. 63.
[37] *Ibid.*, p. 37.
[38] *Ibid.*, p. 65.
[39] *Ibid.*, p. 66.
[40] *Ibid.*, p. 67.

We shall draw some conclusions from these quotes that we have found in the work of Husserl. What is revealed here is that no longer is the moment of living-bodily-presence *the* epistemological and metaphysical moment. In the very description of time it is shown that the present and the past and the future are co-primordial, that is, that the absent is given as co-primordial with the present. Presence and absence are co-constitutive of the real, of being, and the intuition of the living presence is not given without the intuition of absence at the same moment.

How are we to understand this notion of being as absence? What kind of intuition can be had of absence? How are we to think through the co-primordiality of presence and absence as given through time? We do not desire to try to work out fully a meta-physical theory of nonbeing, nor do we hope to give definitive answers to these questions. Much work has already been done particularly by Sartre in *Being and Nothingness*. What we can do, however, is give an indication of where our conclusion concerning Husserl's theory of time leads us, and how it must have an effect on the metaphysics of presence. We are given a clue in the work of Husserl himself, one which comes to the surface in the later works but which he never fundamentally exploits. We can learn to understand being as absence through the notion of *horizon*.

Consider the function of horizons in perception. The landscape, the world as perceived, is always present *with* its horizons; that which is present, which is seen, has also its unseen. It fades into the indeterminate zone which is the visual horizon. The horizon is quasi-present, it is in being certainly, and yet it is not in being the way the perceptual object in front of me is in being. No doubt I can alter my gaze, move closer, and what was the horizon can become the perceptual object, totally present. But not without its own horizon, that indeterminate zone which is the omnipresent *limit* of perceptual being: the beginning of the end of presence. The horizon of the perceptual world is always there, it forms the limit of the spectacle – but it can do so only by being *other* than the spectacle. If the spectacle, the world as visual field, is being as presence, we name this otherness being as absence. And the absent is essential for the apparition of the spectacle; there is no being in the mode of presence without this absence. Together they constitute the being of the spectacle. They are co-primordial.

This way of considering the horizon of the perceptual field is fruitful in that it gives us the most obvious occurrence of horizon for use as a model for the temporal horizon. But there is a more subtle aspect which may be helpful in giving us a model of perceptual horizons that is more useful for understanding the temporal horizon. The notion of horizon just examined has to do with the fading away of presence into the distance; the world as spectacle fades away into the distance which is the horizon. But what of a horizon which is given *nearby*, the horizon that is manifested in what we call lateral vision – what can this teach us about absence?

I am sitting in a chair on my porch, looking up at the trees on a hill in front of me, seeing the houses behind them and the rooftops meeting the sky in the distance as they fade into the horizon. But my gaze does not operate in a straight one-dimensional line; the field of vision opens up as a spread starting at me, unfolding into a sort of triangle with me at the apex. By means of lateral vision I see things to the side of me although they are not in the focus of my attention. I see cars parked up and down the street that runs in front of my house – but not too far. My lateral vision, like direct vision, fades into the horizon at a distance.

If I hold out my arms directly to either side of me I can see my fingertips if I wiggle them. Perhaps I can also see the inside of my elbow-joint. But I cannot see my biceps or my shoulder. At some point between the elbow and the biceps another horizon is inaugurated; it is the horizon of *nearness*. And this horizon of nearness functions in a double fashion; the horizon of the lateral vision is at work not only in the lateral line of vision going outward toward the things at my side, but also at that line which is the "inner limit" toward the back of my head, the fading of the visual field by not being in front of me. This too is a limit of nearness – what is behind me is not the horizon – but there is the horizon as that zone between what is behind and what is in front of me. These are the zones of indeterminateness, the horizons, which are given with and as the conditions of the visual presence.

It is this dyad in its two-dimensional character which is perhaps the better model on which to ground our understanding of the dyad presence-absence in temporality. The future and the past, neither of which are present, are the horizons of the present.

They are also the horizons of the temporal flow as a whole; that unity which we refer to as the flow of time. They are the horizons of the whole temporal flow in the sense of being its outer-limits; the past which can be recalled and the future which can be fore-seen form that indeterminate zone at a distance which is so necessary so that the temporal flow as such can appear as moving toward its horizons in the distance. Time moves toward the future away from the past.

But there is also the horizon to be understood in the sense of nearness, where we take the lateral vision as our model. The future and the past are the near horizons of the present. As such they are the very conditions of the present, contributing to it while not being it. They are not present, they are absent. This is the paradox that faces us. In the phenomenon of retention (and protention, too) Husserl has discovered for us the living experi-ence of absence. To raise the question how do we know, how do we intuit absence, is to raise a false question. The spatial horizon is not given as such; it is given precisely as the horizon of the present spectacle and in the same gaze as the spectacle. The absent is given in the same moment and with the same vision as the present. We do not claim an intuition of absence, direct and unmodified – rather the absent is given only on the ground of the present. We have seen that time is a single moment and that the moments or dimensions of time are co-primordial and together constitute the being of time. As Merleau-Ponty says so well, "in time being and passing are synonymous."[41]

We have seen that for Husserl the temporalizing process is the source of all objectification. And we have shown that at the heart of time lies the co-primordiality of presence and absence. Does this mean that true objectivity needs to be comprehended in the thinking of being as absence no less than being as presence?

According to the epistemological teaching of Husserl, the epistemological moment is the moment of living presence given in intuition, and this is the only possible mode of originary conscious-ness. What we have in fact seen is that all of those terms that are the very meaning of presence for Husserl, "now," "primal im-pression," "living presence," are themselves related to absence.

---

[41] Maurice Merleau-Ponty, *Phenomenology of Perception*, trans. C. Smith (London: Routledge and Kegan Paul, 1962), p. 420.

They are related in the sense that the phenomena described by these terms in fact manifest absence as an essential element of their being. On every one of these levels of the meaning of presence we have seen that presence itself is absence; that is, constituted as presence by absence.

Does this not throw into question the validity of the whole "positivist" epistemology of Husserl? This certainly follows since it is on a "positivist" notion of objective being as full, complete, and exterior to nothingness that Husserl bases his epistemological doctrine. In our first chapter we saw that all the levels of cognition that Husserl considers are founded on the direct presence of the object of intuition to consciousness. We also saw that the evidential vision is the epistemological moment in Husserl's philosophy; this is the model to which all other cognitive functions are subservient.

The notion of evidence was considered in the chapter on language. We found there that it is presence that is the key notion that makes evidence what it is. Evidence is the act that manifests presence as the absolute criterion of knowledge while at the same time being that object of knowledge itself. In short, Husserl's epistemological theory rests on the metaphysics of presence, on the possibility of reducing the absent to a more fundamental presence. It is precisely this possibility which is disallowed by Husserl's phenomenological description of time.

CHAPTER V

INTERSUBJECTIVITY AND
EPISTEMOLOGICAL PRESENCE

> Western philosophy coincides with the unveiling of the Other where the Other in showing itself as being, loses its otherness. From its infancy, philosophy has been filled with the horror of the Other which remains Other, an almost incurable allergy to it. It is because of this that it is essentially a philosophy of being, that the comprehension of being is its last word and the structure of man.[1]

For the final element of our consideration we take our clue from the insight of Levinas. In developing our theme we have seen it is characteristic of the attempt to adhere to the metaphysics of presence that there is an effort to reduce absence to being a converted mode of presence, or at least having presence being more primordial than absence. Another way of saying this is that the metaphysics of presence requires the reduction of otherness to sameness, the making being homogeneous in order that being in the mode of presence be a privileged notion. We maintain that nowhere is this more evident than in the philosophical problematic which is concerned with the Other, with other people, other subjectivities. We shall undertake in this chapter an examination of Husserl's doctrine of intersubjectivity. We shall see that Husserl's teaching on the Other is determined by epistemological considerations. That is, the movement of Husserl's thought is one of reducing the otherness of the Other in order to bring the Other into presence. As Levinas indicates, this is the traditional orientation of Western philosophy. It is precisely at one with the metaphysics of presence.

More and more after *Ideas*, Husserl directs his thoughts to

---

1 Emmanuel Levinas, "On the Trail of the Other," *Philosophy Today*, Spring, 1966, p. 35.

what he feels is a necessary consequence of his phenomenological research – that it be understood as different moments within the context of Transcendental Idealism, and a constitutive idealism at that. He explicitly directs us to read *Ideas* from this standpoint in the "Preface to the English Edition" which he wrote in 1930. In that same preface is a passage which manifests that for Husserl there is a great deal at stake in the question of intersubjectivity; he sees the question of intersubjectivity not as derivative, but as fundamental to his philosophic work:

> The account given in the chapter indicated suffers, as the author confesses, from lack of completeness . . . it lacks what is certainly important to the foundation of this idealism, the proper consideration of the problem of transcendental solipsism or of transcendental intersubjectivity, of the essential relationship of the objective world, that is valid for me and with me.[2]

Husserl often touched on the question of intersubjectivity, but his doctrine was given in its most detailed and accurate form in the *Cartesian Meditations*.[3] We shall limit our exposition to this work. It is in a consideration of Husserl's treatment of the Other that we shall show in this chapter that:

1. In his reflections on the Other, Husserl sees a direct challenge to his epistemological teaching, since the objectivity of the world, and therefore science as such, rests on a foundation of transcendental intersubjectivity. He must therefore have an adequate teaching on the Other if his whole work in epistemology is not going to be nullified.

2. Husserl finds himself in a contradictory situation. He must maintain that on the one hand the Other is intentionally constituted in me, and is therefore present, but on the other hand the Other in his otherness can never be totally present since he too must constitute the world, that is, be "outside" of me, absent from me.

3. Ultimately Husserl's teaching on the Other fails. In maintaining this we are in agreement with many critics – Heidegger, Sartre, Merleau-Ponty, and Levinas. But we shall raise the question as to why it must *necessarily fail within the limits which Husserl*

---

[2] Husserl, *Ideas*, p. 18.
[3] Joseph Kockelmans, *A First Introduction to Husserl's Phenomenology* (Pittsburgh: Duquesne University Press, 1967), p. 230.

sets for himself, and that it is the overriding intention of Husserl to provide an epistemology within the metaphysics of presence that leads to the impossibility of an adequate teaching on the Other. It is the experience that we have of the Other as given in his otherness that flagrantly refutes the metaphysics of presence. In his insistence upon the priority of being in the mode of presence we find that Husserl is forced to reduce the otherness of the Other in order to bring it to presence – and thereby loses the lines of tension necessary to guarantee the objectivity of the world.

4. It is only by accepting the co-primordial status of presence and absence that it becomes possible to give a beginning account of the meaning of the being of the Other.

A. THE REFUTATION OF SOLIPSISM

At the beginning of the Fifth Meditation Husserl poses in the most serious manner an objection which can seemingly be made against phenomenology.[4] Since phenomenology operates within the phenomenological epoché as a transcendentally reduced ego, it must be a transcendental solipsism since the transcendental reduction is restricting to the stream of the ego's pure conscious processes and the unities constituted by their actualities and potentialities.[5] Husserl rejects solipsism as being a logical absurdity. The question then becomes the explication of the experience of the Other in his modes of givenness.

It is clear that to experience another person is not exactly the same as experiencing any other thing of any kind whatsoever: there is a qualitative difference between the comparative experiences of, say, a tree and a person, and of a tree and a house. What is unique about the experience of another person is precisely that it is another person, one like myself who is a *subjectivity.* The Other is experienced as someone who also experiences, and who even experiences me. This is what is involved in the notion that the Other is radically other, manifesting a qualitatively different otherness than that of the general objects of experience which are also other than I, but in no way present themselves in this radical otherness.

4 Husserl, *Cartesian Meditations,* p. 89.
5 *Ibid.*

Thus peculiarly involved with animate organisms, as "psychophysical" Objects, they are *"in" the world*. On the other hand, I experience them at the same time as *subjects for this world*, as experiencing it (this same world that I experience) and, in so doing, experiencing me too, even as I experience the world and others in it.[6]

What is first of all at stake for Husserl, then, is to give an account of how it is possible to encounter this unique object, the object which is also a subject. But tied to this notion of the Other as subject is a second question, one which goes directly to the heart of the epistemology that rests on the functioning of intentional constitution of the world by the transcendental ego. And that is the objectivity of the world. Now, it is true that the objectivity of the world presents a problem for any idealism in general, but it is particularly a problem for Husserl since it is I, this transcendental ego, who constitutes the world as the correlation of my meanings. Thus Husserl was able to say that phenomenology coincides with explicating the concrete ego phenomenologically.[7] However, if there are Others like me then they too must be constituting the world. But it cannot be just any private world, since it is given in experience that I, with Others, constitute a common world, a world which is the ground of our behavior. It is this behavior that shows that it is a common world, for it is the fact that the mutual behavior of the Other and me makes sense that is the ultimate and only proof of the objectivity of the world and that it is not merely the product of my, the constituting ego's dream. For Husserl, to refute the charge of solipsism is to do nothing less than establish the philosophical ground of the objectivity of the world.

Thus the problem is stated at first as a special one, namely that of the "thereness-for-me" of others .... But it soon becomes evident that the range of such a theory is much greater than at first it seems, that it contributes to the founding of a *transcendental theory of the Objective world* .... The existence-sense (*Seinsinn*) of the world and of Nature in particular, as Objective Nature, includes after all, as we have already mentioned, thereness-for-everyone. This is always cointended wherever we speak of Objective reality.[8]

We shall give an account of Husserl's investigation of the intentional constitution of the Other as well as of the Other as *con-*

---

[6] *Ibid.*, p. 91.
[7] *Ibid.*, p. 68.
[8] *Ibid.*, p. 92.

stituting. This account will follow directly the order of development of this doctrine, since the development is ordered by epistemological considerations. The movement of Husserl's thought is consistently determined here by levels and degrees of *presence*, and moves from immediate presence to the transcendental ego to a form of mediate presence. It is the otherness of the Other that is reduced to presence through mediation, thereby reducing absence to presence in the transcendental sphere.

By executing a particular kind of epoché, I eliminate from the thematic field within the transcendental universal sphere all the constitutive activities which are immediately or mediately related to the subjectivity of Others. I thereby reduce the universe of my conscious life to my transcendental sphere of ownness, to my concrete being as a monad. What remains after this abstraction from all relations to other subjectivities is a uniformly connected stratum of the phenomenon "world" which is no longer a world objectively existing for everyone, but belongs peculiarly to me alone, as my private world.[9]

We must explicate the meaning of this unique reduction. Husserl is bringing in "closer" to the constituting ego the source *and* the realm of all meaning. After this reduction, which occurs within the transcendentally reduced sphere, all meaning is in the ego itself, the ego as concrete monad. Ricoeur has the sense of this movement in the following passage:

> Thus, the reduction to the ownness sphere, far from impoverishing experience, leads it from the *cogito* to the *sum* and fulfills the promise, expressed in the Fourth Meditation, of an egology which would set up the ego as monad. By way of an astonishing detour the transcendental, once reduced, reveals being (*être*) as superabundant.[10]

Since all meaning is "in" the ego, what has been achieved is a sphere in which what is, is so in absolute presence. The constituted is totally present to the constituting, and totally accessible, through intentional analysis, to being understood. This is the epistemological moment, the moment of presence. And yet within this sphere there is differentiation in the status of objects as

---

[9] *Ibid.*, pp. 93–98.
[10] Paul Ricoeur, *Husserl: An Analysis of his Phenomenology*, trans. Ballard and Embree (Evanston: Northwestern University Press, 1967), p. 122.

regards a priority of sense. Let us again pick up the flow of Husserl's thought.

There is within my sphere of ownness, among all of the objects pertaining to it, one object uniquely singled-out – my body as an animate organism. It is different because, in accord with my experience of it, I can ascribe fields of sensation to it.[11] If I were to reduce other men as included within my sphere of ownness, I would see bodies. But if I reduce myself as a human being, I perceive myself as a psychophysical unity and this particular, personal ego which functions by means of it in the external world, the world of sensation. I am, however, not reduced to an "empirical ego" since the sphere of ownness itself is possible only within the previously reduced transcendental sphere.[12]

How are we to understand the function of assigning this privileged status to this "psychophysical" object within the reduced sphere of ownness? This object is privileged as that object which is somehow the "closest" of all of the objects of consciousness, with the exception of consciousness itself when it becomes an object for itself. We shall examine later in more detail the notion of "psychophysical unity" and the role it plays for Husserl in the constitution of the Other, but what we want to emphasize here is that this is yet another step in the direction of "nearness" and presence; the ego's body for Husserl is present to consciousness in a very special way, and what makes it special is precisely that it is present, more completely and assuredly present [since it participates in the work of consciousness (perception) itself] than any other object. This notion of the body which Husserl presents here is still part of the movement toward presence, epistemological and ontological. It is still part of the preparation of the grounding of apodicticity whereby Husserl is attempting to anchor consciousness in presence before "going out" toward that which is not apodictically certain, the step which he takes with the introduction of an Other in the perceptual sphere. This begins the reversal of the movement toward presence which we have seen occupies the first seven sections (41–49) of the Fifth Meditation.

If an Other presents himself in my perceptual field (within

[11] Husserl, *Cartesian Meditations*, p. 97.
[12] *Ibid.*, p. 99.

my primordial sphere), I apprehend a body similar to my own, and it must enter into a phenomenal "pairing" association with mine. It is thus that the Other receives a sense appropriated from my body, the sense "animate organism." This sense is given through the sense of my body as animate organism, which sense is given to me in a primordial sense.[13]

We shall return to the notion of pairing shortly, but for now we must see the significance of the reversal of "direction" in the movement of Husserl's thought. The movement toward greater and greater presence has ceased; the object is no longer receiving its sense through *immediate* presence, but rather is receiving it mediately through a kind of "draining off" from that which had itself been given apodictically – my own body. By granting the Other sense through a pairing with my body, Husserl grants it sense by means of a derivation from what is *more present*. Since up until now the movement has been toward presence, toward immediacy, that means that there has been a reversal in the direction in the flow of meaning. And yet it is not to be overlooked that the Other is nonetheless present – it is a secondary, non-originary presence in which the Other is presented. We shall see the consequences of this later in the development of Husserl's thinking.

Verification of the Other's animate organism and governing ego (which are given as a unitary, transcending experience) is given in continual experience.[14] He continues to prove himself as actually an animate organism by his continually harmonious behavior. In this way an Other is constituted appresentatively in my monad as an ego that is not I, but an Other ego which is "mirrored" in my monad.[15] This other ego is not simply given in and of itself, but rather is given as an alter ego. He is another monad who, in his constitutive sense, refers back to me. He is not the same as me or an exact copy however; we are differentiated by the fact that in my monadic sphere the Other always appears in the mode of *there*, whereas my body is always in the absolute *here*.[16] Whatever is appresented in this way is derived from my particular sphere of ownness; it is a coexisting ego in the mode

---

[13] *Ibid.*, pp. 110–11.
[14] *Ibid.*, p. 114.
[15] *Ibid.*, p. 115.
[16] *Ibid.*, p. 116.

there – precisely as alter ego.[17] The other as alter ego must also have his sphere of ownness. It is implicit in the sense of my apperception of the Other that his world, the world belonging to his appearance systems, must be experienced as belonging to the same world belonging to my appearance systems – a mutual objective world – differentiated as *here* and *there*.[18]

That movement "away" from presence which was begun with the initial givenness of the Other's body has been continued and extended here. Contained implicitly in the notion of verification and harmonious behavior is the *span of time*; the Other's behavior occurs across time since it requires a series of behavior for verification. In this sense then the Other is constituted in the past and not only in the present, and here too we can see the movement as a "fading away" from the present.

The main thrust of our attempt to understand this development as a series of stages directly related to presence must focus on the Other as appresented and given as an alter ego. This means that there is yet another mediation required in the presentation of the Other beyond that of the pairing already considered. For the Other must have a sphere of ownness also. In the final analysis that means that the Other is also a subjectivity. It is this which I cannot experience directly. The Other's subjectively never presents itself, makes itself present, for it precisely cannot be constituted in my ego. The only way that Husserl can bring the Other to presence is through a sort of adduction of concordant behavior added on to the imaginative variation of the "here-there." It is this that completes the movement away from presence. Ricoeur capsulizes the movement of thought involved in the constitution of the Other in the Fifth Meditation in a way that supports our interpretation:

Thus, the movement of encroachment by which the sense "ego" is transferred from the original to the analogue is rendered intelligible. The second moment brings the help of a perceptual decipherment of the expression of behavior by which I fulfill the intending of another life. The third moment adds to this reading of the concordances of behavior the fiction "if I were over there." Thus the intending of an alien life progresses from empty to full, without, however, this transgression of my sphere of ownness giving me the subjective life of the other in the original.[19]

[17] *Ibid.*, p. 119.
[18] *Ibid.*, p. 123.
[19] Ricoeur, *Husserl*, pp. 129–130.

There is yet one more stage involved in this effort to under-stand the structure of Husserl's thought as a movement dictated by an epistemological notion tied to the primacy of presence, and that is the final movement to objectivity.

Starting from myself as the original constitutive monad, I appresent other monads (psychophysical subjects). This involves a mutual interrelatedness of my existence and that of all Others, so that my body must be experienced by him (an Other) as his Other.[20] The same is true of all subjects in the community of monads which exists as transcendental intersubjectivity. But of course this transcendental intersubjectivity exists in me, the intending ego.[21] It is in me that it is intentionally constituted, but in such a way that it is the same transcendental intersubjectivity in every constituting consciousness (varying with the sphere of ownness) in his intentional consciousness. Through this con-stitution of transcendental intersubjectivity is executed the con-stitution of a single and uniformly objective world and types of social communities.[22] This being the case, it means that Nature, corporeity, and the psychophysical human being, in the essence of the constitutive sense, are accessible to everyone. Objectivity is community of monads.[23]

We must see the final moment of the movement of Husserl's analysis as being an effort at a kind of recuperation. There is first the final stage of the movement "away" from presence to an intersubjectivity and an intersubjective world, Nature, where seemingly the object maintains a "distance" from the constituting object. But at the final moment Husserl reclaims all of this, as he must, for the transcendental ego active in intentional constitution, and that which has been, as it were, placed at a distance, is once again affirmed as immediately present in the transcendental ego.

In having to carry through contradictory requirements, Hus-serl's doctrine of intersubjectivity and of the objectivity of the world is stretched to unacceptable limits. On the one hand, Husserl has to give an account of the Other and his otherness; on the other hand, he, because of the demands created by the central

---

[20] Husserl, *Cartesian Meditations*, p. 125.
[21] *Ibid.*, p. 124.
[22] *Ibid.*, p. 126.
[23] *Ibid.*, p. 140.

role of the notion of presence in his epistemology, has to bring the Other and his otherness into direct presence, make this Otherness dependent upon presence. From a different perspective Ricoeur indicates this when he says:

> Here the transcendental idealism undergoes a severe test. The existential index which attaches to the Other as "being," then to me as equally "being" Other, finally to separation and fusion as really immanent separation and really immanent unification, appears quite incompatible with the idealistic thesis whereby the Other is constituted "in" me.[24]

We have shown how the movement of Husserl's thought in its entirety makes the doctrine of the Other subservient to the guiding thread of the metaphysics of presence. We have seen that the stages of the thought can all be interpreted as a development within the theme of presence, and how it is this being tied to the "requirement" of presence which leads Husserl into an insoluble dilemma. What we shall now do is examine that explication in the Fifth Meditation which has to be understood as the turning point of Husserl's problematic. We shall show that it is in his attempt to explain the analogical apprehension of the Other that Husserl fails to give a true account of the Other. Rather, he adduces the otherness of the Other, what we shall call the absence of the Other, to presence in an effort to maintain his epistemological and ultimately metaphysical position.

B. THE PRESENCE OF THE OTHER

We have seen that phenomenology is a positivism in the sense that it takes all "positive phenomena" as they appear as the data of all cognition. It is a self-evident datum that the Other appears, and yet there is something problematic about the intentional experience of someone else. Since it seems clear that there is no question but *that* the Other appears, the problematic must have its source in the *mode* of appearance. The problem is simply this: the Other is experienced, but the experience does not have the quality of being originary consciousness the way that the experience of a tree in my perceptual fields is originary consciousness. The Other is not given "in bodily self-presence" as some other perceptual object.

[24] Ricoeur, *Husserl*, p. 136.

Experience is original consciousness; and in fact we generally say, in the case of experiencing a man: the other is himself there before us "in person." On the other hand, this being there in person does not keep us from admitting forthwith that, properly speaking, neither the other Ego himself, nor his subjective processes or his appearances themselves, nor anything else belonging to his own essence, becomes given in our experience originally. If it were, if what belongs to the other's own essence were directly accessible, it would be merely a moment of my own essence, and ultimately he himself and I myself would be the same.[25]

Since the Other is not given, made present through an original experience, he or she is given through a process of mediation. We have already discussed this process of mediation and the role it plays in this problematic in general. Specifically here, this mediation is what Husserl calls "appresentation" or "anological apperception." We are already familiar with this term; apperception is involved in the perceptual intuition in the sensory field in which the front of the object is perceived and the back, the sides, and so on, are apperceived due to the perspectival nature of perception. But Husserl gives the term apperception a new meaning here; in the apperception involved in a perception of a thing of the ordinary kind, the apperceiving intention is in principle always open to fulfillment, to verification. This intuition can achieve the status of *evidence*. In the apperception of the Other the contrary is the case; this intention must in principle always be empty, it can never be fulfilled or verified, "... whereas, in the case of that appresentation which would lead over into the other original sphere, such verification must be excluded *a priori*."[26]

We known that it is an important principle of Husserl that all cognition of a mediated type must be in principle explicable by analysis to an originary presence and intuition. In order to explicate the source which is intuitively original and makes the special appresentation of the Other possible, Husserl brings out the phenomenon of "pairing." Within my sphere of ownness, maintains Husserl, my body is always livingly present, and it is from this living presence that the Other's body gets the sense: "living organism." This giving of sense does not occur on a reflective level of consciousness, nor is it an act of argumentation. Rather, this "pairing" is an analogizing of sense through the institution of sense or meaning.

[25] Husserl, *Cartesian Meditations*, pp. 108–109.
[26] *Ibid.*, p. 109.

> Pairing is a *primal form* of that passive synthesis which we designate as association ... in a pairing association the characteristic feature is that, in the most primitive case, two data are given intuitionally, and with prominence, in the unity of a consciousness and that, on this basis ... as data appearing with mutual distinctness, they found phenomenologically a unity of similarity and are thus always constituted precisely as a pair.[27]

What is Husserl attempting to establish here? On the one hand, it is clear that the Other cannot be given in an originary intuition since this would require the possibility of absolute presence, in this case the reduction of the very sense of the Other, the otherness, to sameness. It is for this reason that Husserl must understand the Other to be given through a type of apperception, and one which is in principle never open to the fulfilling intuitions which are in principle necessary in the apperception of a thing. Even though a thing transcends me, it nevertheless has its sense, its meaning constituted by me and it can continually be brought into presence. A thing has its sense constituted by me, it precisely *does not* have the characteristic of otherness. On the other hand, however, in keeping with the epistemology that Husserl intends, it is necessary for the Other to be accessible in an act of originary consciousness. This demand lies at the heart of the analysis of analogizing apperception which is to be legitimatized by "pairing."

The pair is given in an original intuition, although in fact it is only one member of the pair (my body) that is given in an originary intuition. Husserl himself realizes the shortcomings of this doctrine and attempts to resolve the difficulty through the distinction of "here-there" as previously mentioned. But this too fails as can be seen in the description by Husserl himself:

> It (the Other's ego) is therefore conceivable only as an analogue of something included in my peculiar ownness. Because of its sense-constitution it occurs necessarily as an "intentional modification" of that Ego of mine .... In other words, another monad becomes constituted appresentatively in mine.[28]

The failure of the "here-there" which differentiates the Other from myself occurs because it again leads back to seeing the Other as an intentional modification of my ego. That is, the distinction

---

[27] *Ibid.*, p. 112.
[28] *Ibid.*, p. 115.

is constituted precisely *by me*. We agree with the thesis of Ricoeur that this failure is inevitable.

> Right up to the end the descriptive spirit and the requirement of constitution tend to meet but fail to blend into each other, for according to the idealistic requirement of constitution, the Other must be a modification of my ego and according to the realistic character of description, the Other never ceases to exclude himself from the sphere of "my monad." [29]

We concur, but within the limits of our problematic we offer the interpretation that the idealism of Husserl is dependent on a more primitive notion, the metaphysics of presence. What Ricoeur attributes to idealism we attribute to an epistemology which has as its source the guiding intention of the metaphysics of presence, and we maintain that it is the requirement of the metaphysics of presence that comes into conflict with the descriptive spirit of phenomenology. Husserl's idealism must be understood as being a function, a necessary outgrowth of that doctrine which we call the metaphysics of presence. And it is here that we must locate the source of Husserl's failure at resolving the problematic of intersubjectivity.

C. THE BEING OF THE OTHER

We can turn to the work of Sartre to pick up an insight of how it is possible to think through the problematic of intersubjectivity on the basis of a philosophy other than that of the metaphysics of presence, even though we are by no means claiming than an adequate resolution of the problem is presented in his work. What is of interest to us in the work of Sartre is that he realizes full well that to understand the being of the Other it must be possible to understand it as an *extra-mundane* being, for it is only in this way that the Other can have the status of being Other, of being other than merely intended in me. The term "extra-mundane" here is telling in terms of the positivist philosophy of Husserl, since what is unique about the Other is that he or she cannot be "grasped" in a positive intuition as can all of the other subjects of experience, according to Husserl. Just as in the doctrine on temporality, Husserl's teaching on the Other fails because he maintains the priority of presence to absence,

[29] Ricoeur, *Husserl*, p. 130.

rather than accept the co-primordiality of being in the mode of absence with being in the mode of presence. Sartre remarks on just this when he analyzes Husserl's failure to "get to" the being of the Other.

> Moreover Husserl understood this since he says that "the Other" as he is revealed to our concrete experience is an *absence*. But within Husserl's philosophy, at least, how can one have a full intuition of an absence? [30]

The being of the Other is a radical transcendence and can therefore, like the flow of time, be understood only through a grasping of the co-primordiality of presence and absence, for the Other is both. Only as absent can the Other retain the extra-mundane character that is necessary to maintain the notion of otherness in its real sense. This means that only in a philosophy in which absence can have a co-primordial status with presence can the being of the Other be treated in a manner that does not necessarily reduce otherness to an object in presence. This is not possible within the framework of the metaphysics of presence and that epistemology for which presence is the measure of being. That Others are other than I means that their meanings are not to be found in my world, a concatenation of my meanings and intentions. The beings who are radically Other are not dependent upon my knowledge nor my meanings. They are given *as* intending, as the source of meanings, and not as encompassed objects-meant. Their being is other than my own; it cannot be given in the totality of my world waiting to be revealed. Rather, they have their being across the world, giving meaning to the world as being co-primordial with my own. It is only on this ground that we can approach the being of the Others.

We have seen that the very unfolding of the movement of Husserl's reflection on the problematic of intersubjectivity can be understood as an effort to secure knowledge of the Other apodictically on the foundation of presence. This movement reveals the contradictory nature of the requirements that Husserl feels he must satisfy for his transcendental idealism. On the one hand, he must maintain that I, as the transcendental ego, constitute the Other intentionally; therefore his or her being is present "in" me. On the other hand, the being of the Other cannot be totally

[30] Sartre, *Being and Nothingness*, p. 234.

present in me nor dependent upon me since he or she too must constitute the objective world. It is through thinking the Other as absent, but yet more primordially present, that we come upon the notion of apperception to account for the experience of the Other as originary consciousness. But this solution is inadequate since it too depends upon the sense of the otherness of the Other being constituted in me.

Finally, we have seen that this problematic of intersubjectivity must remain unresolved within the epistemological and metaphysical limits that Husserl sets for himself. His idealism manifests his adherence to the metaphysics of presence, the notion of the priority of being in the mode of presence. What the experience of the Other in fact teaches us is that the being of the Other remains inexplicable so long as presence holds a metaphysical priority and dominates philosophical thinking. This means, as Merleau-Ponty said: "What is interesting is not an expedient to solve the 'problem of the other' – it is a transformation of the problem." [31]

[31] Maurice Merleau-Ponty, *The Visible and the Invisible*, trans. A. Lingis (Evanston: Northwestern University Press, 1968), p. 269.

CHAPTER VI

CONCLUSION
Philosophy as the Servant of Humanity

A. REVIEW OF OUR FINDINGS

The phenomenology of Edmund Husserl is in conformity with, and an outgrowth of, that traditional orientation of Western philosophy that we call the metaphysics of presence. This becomes manifest in the development of Husserl's epistemological teaching. We have also maintained, however, that in certain of Husserl's greatest phenomenological themes and descriptions he has contradicted, despite his intentions, this guiding notion of the primacy of the notion of presence; he has revealed instead the necessity for comprehending the co-primordiality of presence and absence.

It is in working out the intuitionist doctrine presented in *Ideas* in light of the above thesis that we see the efficacy of the metaphysics of presence on the level of epistemology by seeing the priveleged position that being in the mode of presence holds ontologically as well as epistemologically. At the heart of Husserl's work is the development of an epistemology, and that development is consistently and constantly determined by the notion of presence as the epistemological moment. The presence of the epistemological object of consciousness to consciousness in evidential vision is the epistemological moment because it is the moment of presence, and therefore the absolute foundation of all cognition.

A major break is made from the traditional positivism by Husserl through his doctrine concerning the intuition of essence. Unlike all previous teachings grounded in empiricism or positivism, Husserl makes the claim that essences can be the object of direct intuition – eidetic intuition – and that therefore eidetic intuition serves as an original source of knowledge. Thereby Husserl goes beyond the claim of positivism precisely on the grounds of positivism itself, since essences are positive phenomena which are given in primordial dator intuitions.

Through his phenomenological research Husserl shows that it is the nature of the sensible thing, as well as the nature of perception, that the thing is never perceived "absolutely," but rather that it gives itself in perception as an infinite possible series of profiles, as *Abshattungen*. By this understanding Husserl shows the claim of scepticism to be an empty objection and returns perception to its rightful place in the cognitive order. Intuition is the absolute foundation of all knowledge. The work of intuition, and the highest epistemological moment, is the bringing of the object to presence in "bodily self-presence" within the phenomenological sphere. The phenomenological reduction makes it possible that there is a sphere of being totally present to consciousness, totally accessible to consciousness, in which being is absolutely present. That sphere of being is consciousness itself.

This teaching is the epistemological manifestation of that very traditional metaphysical doctrine that we have named the metaphysics of presence. To Husserl it must surely have seemed that he had resolved a fundamental problematic that has haunted the metaphysics of presence throughout its development – the problematic of the "proof" of the claim that the moment of presence *is* the moment of being and that the moment of presence of consciousness to being is, correlatively, the moment of truth. That is, it has always been somewhat questionable as to how that doctrine could justify itself as a doctrine. In short, how could it provide for itself an epistemological foundation grounded in self-evidence? This is the question that Husserl thinks through with the idea of science and the foundation of the sciences and the ultimate understanding of phenomenology as a phenomenology of reason.

All sciences – those in the category of the sciences of fact as well as those of the sciences of the essence – have their foundation and ultimate justification or verification in or through intuition. This is of course really just a strong positivism, something which is itself a manifestation of the metaphysics of presence. But how do we know that, how can we be certain that these

sciences are solidly grounded? We know it because they have
their foundation in a more primary science – phenomenology –
which is the only science that deals with the region of being in
which intuition is given – the region of consciousness. It is within
consciousness as an ultimate region of being that we find phenomenology as the science that provides its own foundation, since it
is the only science in which verification is given in its meaning.
And the highest moment of verification – and therefore the
grounding of all science whatsoever – is the presence of evidence
in consciousness. The evidential vision is the highest work of
consciousness, both epistemologically and ontologically, since
that is the moment in which consciousness is totally present to
itself.

The evidential vision as the epistemological moment is not
enough in itself to constitute evidence. For Husserl the notion
of evidence is inextricably tied up with expression. Evidence is for
Husserl the highest or absolute form of verification, and verification is related to systems of science and of knowledge. They in
turn are related to meanings, expressions, logic, in short, language.

The phenomenological research of Husserl begins with and
grows out of his work with language and the relation that holds
between language and epistemology. Husserl's thought here has a
double movement: first there is the relation between the expression and the meaning, the sign and the signified, and then as an
extra-essential but phenomenologically united factor, the fulfillment of the meaning-intention through an intuition. Intuition is
required in the accomplishment of evidence, but so is signification,
and the act of signification depends upon the act of the constitution of signs as well as the constitution of meanings. It is for
this reason that Husserl needs to provide a twofold understanding
of the nature of consciousness. Consciousness must be understood
as functioning in the mode of interpretation, as well as in the mode
of representation, if Husserl is to account for these two diverse
requirements in the constitution of language.

For Husserl language has the notion of evidence at its limits;
the theory of language is structured in such a way as to meet the
task of providing for a theory of evidence. But the whole theory
of evidence itself is profoundly determined by the metaphysics of
presence since the whole notion of evidence that Husserl holds is

possible only on the supposition of the priority of being in the mode of presence as the epistemological and metaphysical absolute. And this means that the theory of language is structured in accord with the determinations that emanate from this dominating idea rather than from the demands of language itself. This is the source of the uneasy duality of the working consciousness that Husserl projects in order to account for the functioning of language. Husserl is forced to reduce much of the phenomenon of language. He ignores its density, that relationship that language has with itself in the constitution of meaning, because this would require a teaching in which absence could be co-primordial with presence, and would therefore be in direct conflict with the metaphysics of presence.

Husserl himself seems to have had an awareness of some sort in this direction since in his later works he transforms the meaning of the function of evidence to be that of an ideal limit rather than the immediate possibility that it is portrayed as in the *Logische Untersuchungen*. That is, it is in evidence itself that in some way absence is always at the border of presence. But although he constantly revises the teaching on evidence, Husserl never really goes back to rethink the question of language, and this teaching remains fundamentally the same, permeated through and through with the limiting concepts of the metaphysics of presence which exclude the possibility of the constitution of meaning through absence as well as presence. This in turn prevents language from being understood as a system of meanings that get part of their meaning from the relations of the system itself. With a new understanding of language could come a new understanding of the concept of evidence, one that would take into account the co-primordial status of absence and presence.

Husserl's research on temporality provides the revelation that in time is given the co-primordiality of absence and presence in the form of past-present-future as necessarily unified. It is against the express intentions of Husserl that this is the understanding that he renders of time; what he really sets out to do is to unfold all of the moments of time from the notion of the "primordial now," the "living now" that serves as the generation of all presence. It is in his teaching on time that much of Husserl's adherence to the doctrine of the primacy of presence becomes very much clarified since it comes to the surface in such notions as the "living now," "primal impression," and "bodily self-presence." These concepts of temporality are the very meaning of presence for Husserl, and it is through these concepts that he attempts to found his teaching on time.

But a careful reading of the phenomenological description of time renders a very different understanding from the one that Husserl intended; what Husserl in fact shows is that the past, in the mode of retention, and the future, in the mode of protention, are given *with* the present as co-primordial moments. But of course they are not given as present, but precisely as absent. That means that Husserl himself has shown that absence and presence are co-primordial; they arise at one moment, together, and therefore presence has no priority of being. This is of course in direct opposition to the teaching of the metaphysics of presence, that teaching which works on the principle of the primacy of being in the mode of presence and attempts to reduce the alien, the absent, nothingness, nonbeing, to a derivative and secondary mode of being.

And if Husserl himself did not understand this, those who followed him certainly did. There is no question but that the teaching on time that Husserl gives lies at the root of the three great existentialist thinkers, Heidegger, Sartre, and Merleau-Ponty. It is certainly no accident that the ontologies of these three thinkers break away from the metaphysics of presence to embrace ontological doctrines based on the co-primordiality of presence and absence. And at the heart of their teachings, and at the heart of phenomenology lies Husserl's phenomenological description of time. It is there that the definitive break is made with the metaphysics of presence.

It is in his teaching on intersubjectivity that Husserl most clearly reveals that he is bound by and to the requirements of the metaphysics of presence, for it is here that he clearly makes the effort of reducing the alien to the given, the absent to the present, the other to sameness. But again it is Husserl himself who brings this to light by articulating very conscientiously the problems concerning "pairing" and "apperception" as the mode in which the Other is given.

The sense of the Other as Other, as also a constituting ego, must come through the revelation of the Other as a psychophysical organism and this sense can come only through a kind of transference from myself as a psychophysical organism. It is in this way that Husserl hopes to account for the knowledge that I have of the alter ego. But of course the Other also has to be not me, and has not to derive his or her being, his or her meaning, from my own, since it is only as Other that the Other too can constitute the world and thereby guarantee its objectivity.

If Husserl is trapped in a kind of solipsism it is not because he does not recognize the danger. Husserl works very diligently to escape this philosophical solipsism, but in the end he must fail, since the very meaning of the Other must be constituted in and by me, as the transcendental constituting ego in the Husserlean scheme of things. But this is to deny the radical otherness of the Other, for the meaning of the Other is that he or she constitutes him or herself as well as the world together with me. It is here that the requirements of the metaphysics of presence bring Husserl to an insoluble impasse; the otherness of the Other must be given in an original intuition since that is the epistemological determination of the metaphysics of presence. But in order to do that, I must bring the Other to presence, and to accomplish that means to reduce the alien, the Other, to sameness. That is to lose the very sense of the Other that I am trying to grasp.

What is clear is that it is only on the grounds of an ontology that allows for a co-primordiality of absence with presence that it becomes possible to speak of the Other in his otherness. And this means, within the phenomenological framework, that it is only as open to the possibility of the otherness of the Other that we can begin to understand the notion of an objective world, one constituted by all, shared by all, and made meaningful by all. The Others give themselves – but not as mine. So too with the world.

B. PHENOMENOLOGY AND THE POSSIBILITY OF HISTORY

We have made examinations and drawn some conclusions. At the end of those chapters that dealt with time, language, and intersubjectivity we have given indications, suggestions, and reflections concerning the direction for pursuing these topics that come out of this research. We do not, of course, claim originality or even that we made innovations; much of the work has already begun. We less determine a new direction than articulate one already in motion and perhaps clarify its relation to the old path. What then is left to do?

Coincidentally, or perhaps not, we turn our attention to that same topic that engrossed Husserl in his last works – the question of a philosophy of history. Husserl takes up this topic in the same book in which he brings the notion of the Lebenswelt to the fore, the famous *Crisis of European Science and Transcendental Phenomenology*. We agree with Paul Ricoeur that the fundamental philosophical ground of the question of the meaning and accessibility of history is already at work in the *Cartesian Meditations*.

> One can well say that the entire enigma of a history which includes its own including – that is, I, the one who understands, who wills, who makes the sense of this history – was already taken up in the theory of *Einfuelung* (sympathy or experience of the Other).[1]

It is not our task here to examine the teaching of Husserl on history. In a sense this would involve a redundancy of effort since we already have scrutinized three topics – language, time, and Otherness – that lie at the core of history. And it is in terms of these three that the intelligibility of history must be brought to the fore.

Husserl joins Hegel in thinking history as the development of the Idea. This is in keeping with the traditional Greek thinking on the matter of history. It is not accidental that the Greeks had no philosophy of history; that they felt that the muse of poetry was higher than the muse of history since it was more universal. Therefore the "stuff" of history was such that it was not really the business of philosophy. Within the teaching of the metaphysics of presence a real philosophy of history that takes the "stuff" of history to be anything other than the Idea is impossible, since it is only the Idea that can be brought to total presence, that is, made intelligible, and this intelligibility, this presence, is the metaphysical moment.

By abandoning what is perhaps the oldest philosophical inclination – the metaphysics of presence – we shall find repercussions on every level of the philosophic enterprise. If, as we have shown is indicated by the work of Husserl himself, presence does

---

[1] Ricoeur, *Husserl*, pp. 172–3.

not have primacy but is rather co-primordial with absence, then the thought that history is the history of the Idea falls, and it becomes necessary to rethink the entire problematic. By taking absence and presence as co-primordial elements given as necessary for the comprehension of being, we are forced to abandon also the notion of philosophy as the contemplation of the Idea. And it indeed becomes *necessary* to raise these questions, since, as Husserl says so simply: "We are ... through our philosophical activity the servants of humanity."[2]

If history ceases to be the unfolding of the Idea and becomes instead the diverse intermingling of elements both present and absent, then the philosophy of history can respond to a twofold absence – the future and the self-conscious comprehension of the mass of humanity.

The meaning of the past is not yet settled. That meaning is not present because it is not carried as an idea since history is not the unfolding of the Idea. The meaning of the past is determined not only in terms of the past and present, but equally in the future, the absent, the not yet. As such, the making of history becomes a *task*. The task and the struggle to accomplish the task become the source of meaning along with the events and movements of the past. In this way history becomes meaningful through both presence and absence; history is both the accomplishment and the task.

How is this notion of history related to philosophy other than by the effort of understanding the notion, since philosophy does deal with understanding? We do not claim that making history is the work of philosophy – it is not, at least not directly. The work of philosophy is the development of the understanding of the meaning of history. And that includes the understanding of the task that is history. That understanding is of and for those who make history – the mass of humanity.

The contemplation of the Idea is for the few – the task of making history belongs to the many. It is from this task that philosophy, after the overthrow of the metaphysics of presence, must find its purpose. Its purpose is no longer the contemplation of the Idea but the understanding of the human condition. No

---

[2] *Ibid.*, p. 167.

longer leading the few to the presence of being, but bringing self-consciousness to the many, the makers of history. If we can comprehend this understanding of philosophy we can perhaps grasp the true significance for each philosopher of what was said by a certain philosopher: "The philosophers have only *interpreted* the world differently, the point is, to *change* it."

BIBLIOGRAPHY

ARISTOTLE. *The Basic Works of Aristotle*, ed. and intro. by R. McKeon. NewYork: Random House, 1941.

DERRIDA, JACQUES. *Speech and Phenomena*, and Other Essays on Husserl's Theory of Signs, trans. D. Allison. Evanston: Northwestern University Press, 1973.

FARBER, MARVIN. *The Foundations of Phenomenology*, 3rd ed. revised. Albany: The Research Foundation of the State University of New York, 1967.

FUCHS, JO-ANN. "The Philosophy of Language of Maurice Merleau-Ponty." Unpublished Master's Thesis, The Pennsylvania State University, University Park, Pennsylvania, 1968.

HEIDEGGER, MARTIN. *Being and Time*, trans. Macquarrie and Robinson. New York: Harper and Row, 1962.

HUSSERL, EDMUND. *Cartesian Meditations*, trans. D. Cairns. The Hague: Martinus Nijhoff, 1964.

HUSSERL, EDMUND. *Ideas: General Introduction to Pure Phenomenology*, trans. Gibson. London: George Allen and Unwin, Ltd., 1931.

HUSSERL, EDMUND. *Logical Investigations*, 2 vols., trans. J.N. Findlay. New York: Humanities Press, 1970.

HUSSERL, EDMUND. *The Idea of Phenomenology*, trans. Alston and Nakhnikien. The Hague: Martinus Nijhoff, 1964.

HUSSERL, EDMUND. *Phenomenology of Internal Time Consciousness*, ed. Heidegger, trans. J. Churchill, intro. by Schragg. Bloomington: Indiana University Press, 1964.

KANT, IMMANUEL. *Critique of Pure Reason*, trans. N.K. Smith. New York: St. Martin's, 1965.

KOCKELMANS, JOSEPH. *A First Introduction to Husserl's Phenomenology*. Pittsburgh: Duquesne University Press, 1967.

LAUER, QUENTIN. *Phenomenology: Its Genesis and Prospect*. New York: Harper and Row, 1965.

LEVINAS, EMMANUEL. "On the Trail of the Other," *Philosophy Today*, Spring, 1966, pp. 34–35.

MERLEAU-PONTY, MAURICE. *Phenomenology of Perception*, trans. C. Smith. London: Routledge and Kegan Paul, 1962.

MERLEAU-PONTY, MAURICE. *Signs*, trans. with intro. by R. McCleary. Evanston: Northwestern University Press, 1964.

MERLEAU-PONTY, MAURICE. *The Visible and Invisible*, ed. Lefort, trans. A. Lingis. Evanston: Northwestern University Press, 1968.

RICOEUR, PAUL. *Husserl: An Analysis of his Phenomenology*, trans. Ballard and Embree. Evanston: Northwestern University Press, 1967.

SARTRE, JEAN-PAUL. *Being and Nothingness*, trans. H. Barnes. New York: Philosophical Library, 1953.